NAZI GERMANY

STEPHEN LEE

GW00363271

HEINEMANN
EDUCATIONAL

Heinemann Educational Ltd
a division of Heinemann Educational Books Ltd
Halley Court, Jordan Hill, Oxford OX2 8EJ

OXFORD   LONDON   EDINBURGH
MADRID   ATHENS   BOLOGNA
MELBOURNE   SYDNEY   AUCKLAND
IBADAN   NAIROBI   GABORONE   HARARE
KINGSTON   PORTSMOUTH (NH)   SINGAPORE

First published 1989
Reprinted 1990

British Library Cataloguing in Publication Data

Lee, Stephen
　Nazi Germany
　1. Germany 1918–1945
　I. Title
　943.085

ISBN 0-435-31036-4

Designed and produced by
The Pen & Ink Book Company Ltd, Huntingdon

Printed in Great Britain by Scotprint, Edinburgh

Acknowledgements

The author and publisher would like to thank the following for
permission to reproduce photographs on the pages indicated:

BBC Hulton Picture Library: pp. 7, 10, 40 (lower right) and 60;
Bilderdienst Süddeutscher Verlag: pp. 4, 5, 9, 11, 12, 18, 19, 20, 29,
30 (lower right), 31, 32, 33, 37, 39, 42, 55 (top left) and 63 (top right);
Bundesarchiv, Koblenz: p. 30 (lower left); Keystone Collection: pp.
14 and 23 (lower right); Library of Congress: p. 56; Mansell
Collection: p. 61 (top right); Popperfoto: pp. 8, 23 (top), 24 (lower
left), 36, 46 (top), 55 (top right), 59 and 61 (lower right); Ullstein
Bilderdienst: pp. 16, 17, 21, 25, 26, 34, 38, 40 (lower left and top
right), 41, 43, 45, 46 (lower), 47, 48, 49, 53, 54, 57, 58, 62 and 63 (top
left).

Details of Written Sources

In some sources the wording or sentence structure has been
simplified to make sure that the source is accessible.

N. H. Baynes (ed.), *The Speeches of Adolf Hitler*, Oxford 1942: 1.5B,
2.3E, 2.3F
C. Bielenberg, *The Past is Myself*, Chatto and Windus 1968: 2.12E,
3.2E
E. Amy Buller, *Darkness over Germany*, Longman 1945: 2.6H
A. Bullock, *Hitler: A Study in Tyranny*, Penguin 1969: 2.3G
Daily Express 1936: 2.12A
Deutsche Zeitung, 28 June, 1919: 1.2G
Documents concerning German-Polish Relations and the Outbreak
of Hostilities between Great Britain and Germany on September 3,
1939, HMSO: 3.2A, 3.2D
Documents on German Foreign Policy, HMSO 1949: 3.3C
T. Edwards, *Hitler and Germany*, History Broadsheets Heinemann
Educational 1972: 2.4D, 2.10G
Encounter, July 1961: 3.3F
J. Fest, *Hitler*, Weidenfeld & Nicolson 1974: 3.8C
The Brown Book of the Hitler Terror, Gollancz 1933: 2.2C
J. A. S. Grenville, *The Major International Treaties 1914–1973*,
Methuen 1974: 3.2C

R. Grunberger, *A Social History of the Third Reich*, Weidenfeld &
Nicolson 1971: 2.5E, 2.10E, 3.7D
C. W. Guillebaud, *The Economic Recovery of Germany from 1933 to
Incorporation of Austria in March 1938*, Macmillan 1939: 2.10A
S. William Halperin, *Germany Tried Democracy*, New York 1965:
1.2E
Hansard, 1919: 1.2F
Adolf Hitler, *Mein Kampf* (1924 trans. R. Mannheim) Sentry
Paperbacks 1943: 1.7B, 1.7E, 2.5B, 3.3A
Adolf Hitler, *Second Book*, New York 1962: 1.7F, 3.3B
W. Hoffer, *Der Nationalsozialismus*, trans. C. Fox, Frankfurt 1957:
2.4B
T. L. Jarman, *The Rise and Fall of Nazi Germany*, New York
University Press 1956: 2.2F
A. B. Keith, *Speeches and Documents on International Affairs*, Oxford
University Press 1938: 1.2B, 2.8A
J. M. Keynes, *The Economic Consequences of the Peace*, Macmillan
1919: 1.2H
H. Krausnick, *The Anatomy of the SS State*, London 1968: 2.4C
W. Laqueur (ed.), *A Dictionary of Politics*, Weidenfeld & Nicolson
1971: 2.2G
The League of Nations Official Journal, Special Supplement 44: 1.6B
R. Leonhard, *A Fairy Tale of Christmas*, (trans. J. Cleugh): 1.8C
K. Ludecke, *I Knew Hitler*, London 1938: 1.4C, 1.5E
W. Maser, *Hitler's Letters and Notes*, Heinemann 1974: 3.3D, 3.8B
M. Montgelas, *The Case for the Central Powers* (trans. C. Vesey),
Allen & Unwin 1925: 1.2C
G. Mosse, *Nazi Culture*, W. H. Allen 1966: 2.6F
A. Nevins and H. S. Commager, *The Pocket History of the United
States*, New York 1956: 3.5C
News Chronicle, 2 July 1934: 2.3H
H. Nicolson, *Peacemaking 1919*, New York 1939: 1.2D
J. Noakes and G. Pridham (eds.), *Documents on Nazism 1919–1945*
Cape 1974: 1.4B, 1.4E, 1.5C, 1.9C, 2.7C, 2.7D, 2.8D, 2.9B, 2.9C,
2.9D, 2.9E, 2.11A, 2.11F, 2.11G, 2.12B, 3.2B, 3.6A
R. O'Neill, *The German Army and the Nazi Party*, Cassell 1966: 2.3C
Von Papen, *Memoirs*, Deutsch 1952: 1.8F
Purnell, *History of the Twentieth Century*, BPC Publishing Ltd 1969:
2.3B
H. Rauschning, *Hitler Speaks*, Thornton Butterworth 1939: 2.3D
J. Remak, *The Nazi Years*, Prentice-Hall 1969: 1.8A, 2.1C, 2.1D,
2.4A, 2.5C, 2.5F, 2.7B, 2.7F, 2.11B, 2.11D, 2.12C, 3.7A, 3.7B
Schools Council General Studies Project, *Nazi Education*, Longman
1972: 2.6B, 2.6A
P. Scheidemann, *The Making of New Germany: Memoirs*, (trans. J. E.
Mitchell), New York 1929: 1.1B
L. L. Snyder, *The Weimar Republic*, Van Nostrand 1966: 1.1D
A. J. P. Taylor, *Origins of the Second World War*, London 1963: 3.3G
The United States Strategic Bombing Survey, Overall Report,
Washington 1945: 3.7E
The Von Hassell Diaries, 1938–44, London 1948: 2.12A
Nazi Conspiracy and Aggression: Opinion and Judgement, Washington
1947: 3.3E, 3.6D
Sir J. Wheeler-Bennett, *The Nemesis of Power*, Macmillan 1953: 2.1C

For Charlotte

CONTENTS

1.1 THE BEGINNING OF THE WEIMAR REPUBLIC, 1918–1?

Confusion and chaos in Germany

Germany had been involved in the **First World War** since 1914. By November 1918 it was losing on the western front to Britain, France and the United States. The German people were short of food, and dissatisfaction spread throughout the country against the German Emperor, or **Kaiser**. Soldiers mutinied in German ports such as Kiel and Hamburg, and the whole country was threatened with upheaval.

On 9 November 1918 the Kaiser abdicated and fled to Holland. On that same day, one of the leaders of the **Social Democratic Party**, Philipp Scheidemann, declared from a window in the Reichstag (Parliament) building in Berlin that Germany was now a **republic**. You can see a photograph of this event (Source A) and read the end of his speech (Source B). Two days later, on 11 November, the new Republic signed an armistice with the Allies.

But the disturbances continued. At first the Republic was ruled by moderate left-wingers, the Social Democrats. They were challenged by parties which were on the extreme left. The most important of these was the **Spartacus League**, under Rosa Luxemburg and Karl Liebknecht, which aimed to set up a communist state similar to that in the Soviet Union. Source C shows a Spartacist leader addressing a crowd. This sort of activity worried the Social Democrats so much that they did a deal with the army which enabled them to put down two series of Spartacist demonstrations early in 1919. Several thousand people were killed in Berlin, including Luxemburg and Liebknecht. At the same time a Soviet (or Communist) republic was also toppled in Bavaria. It seemed that the moderates had won – at least for the time being.

A new constitution, 1919

In January 1919 elections were held throughout Germany. The Reichstag could not meet in Berlin because of the street violence involving the Spartacists. Instead, the authorities

SOURCE B

'Workmen and soldiers realize the historic importance of today. Miracles have happened. Long and incessant toil is before us. Nothing must be done that brings dishonour to the labour movement. Stand united and loyal and be conscious of your duty. The old and rotten – the monarchy – has broken down. Long live the new! Long live the German Republic!'

The conclusion of Scheidemann's speech.

SOURCE A

◀ *Scheidemann proclaiming Germany a republic, 9 November 1918.*

SOURCE C

Spartacist meeting.

used the city of **Weimar**, which gave its name to the new Republic even after the Reichstag moved back to Berlin later in 1919. By August 1919 a **new constitution** had been drawn up. This made Germany one of the most democratic countries in the world. You can see some of the terms in Source D.

All Germans over the age of 20 had the vote, and the Reichstag was elected by **proportional representation** (that is, each party gained a number of seats in proportion to its total vote). The head of the government was the **Chancellor**, who needed the support of over half the Reichstag. The head of state was the **President**, who was elected by the people every seven years. Normally the President did not play a part in everyday politics, leaving the details to the Chancellor. However, the time might come when there was an emergency. In this case, the President could suspend parts of the constitution and rule by special powers.

In many ways the German people were very fortunate to exchange the Kaiser for a new democracy. Unfortunately, this democracy had two weaknesses which were to cause serious problems for the Republic in the future.

First, the use of proportional representation in elections meant that no political party ever had a majority in the Reichstag. Governments were therefore made of up different parties; these were called **coalitions**. The Republic was usually run by coalitions between the Social Democrats, the People's Party, the Democratic Party and the Centre Party. These worked quite well when times were good, but major splits would occur between them as soon as there was a crisis.

Second, the only person who could govern effectively in such a crisis was the President. By using article 48 of the constitution he could take on special powers; this meant that he was actually suspending Germany's democracy. As we shall see, this happened after 1929, following an economic crisis known as the Great Depression.

SOURCE D

'The German Reich is a Republic. Political authority comes from the people' (article 1).

'The delegates (in the Reichstag) are elected by universal, equal, direct and secret suffrage by men and women over twenty years of age, according to proportional representation' (article 22).

'In the event that the public order and security are seriously disturbed or endangered, the Reich President may take the measures necessary for their restoration, intervening, if necessary, with the aid of the armed forces' (article 48).

'The Chancellor and the Ministers require for the exercise of their office the confidence of the Reichstag' (article 54).

Extracts from the Weimar Constitution.

EVIDENCE

1.2 THE TREATY OF VERSAILLES

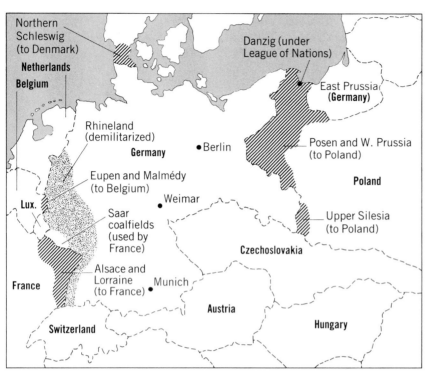

◄ *German territorial losses in 1919.*

▨ Removed from Germany as result of the Treaty of Versailles

On 28 June 1919 a German delegation signed the **Treaty of Versailles** in the Hall of Mirrors at Versailles Palace. This had been drawn up by **President Wilson** of the United States, the British Prime Minister **Lloyd George** and the French leader **Clemenceau**.

Germany was blamed for starting the First World War (see Source A). The map shows the **territory** lost by Germany to its neighbours. Germany gave up Alsace and Lorraine to France, Eupen and Malmédy to Belgium, and Posen and West Prussia to Poland. In some areas the inhabitants were given the opportunity to vote (in plebiscites) for whether they wanted to remain in Germany or join a neighbouring state. Upper Silesia chose Poland, and Northern Schleswig voted for Denmark. Germany also lost all its **overseas colonies**; these were given to the victors to look after as 'mandates' or territories under trust.

Also, Germany was expected to pay **reparations**, or compensation for the damage caused during the war. These reparations were fixed in 1921 at 136,000 million German marks. Finally, Germany was prevented from being a military power in the future. The Rhineland was to be **demilitarized** and the German army limited to 100,000. There was to be no air force, and only six battleships were allowed to the navy.

Was this treatment fair?

This unit has a variety of sources providing a range of different views on the Treaty of Versailles. All of them are **primary sources**; that is, they were produced during the period with which they deal. Each has a different comment to make or is written from a different standpoint.

'The Allied Governments affirm, and Germany accepts, the responsibility of Germany and her allies for causing all the losses and damage to which the Allied Governments and peoples have been subjected as a result of the War.'

Article 231 of the Treaty of Versailles.

'Germany pursued no aim either in Europe or elsewhere which could only be achieved by means of war.'

The German reply to Source A, 1925.

'If I am returned (to Parliament), Germany is going to pay. I personally have no doubt that we will get everything that you can squeeze out of a lemon and a bit more.'

Sir Eric Geddes in a British election speech, 1918.

SOURCE D

'Now that we see them (the terms) as a whole, we realize that they are much too stiff. The real crime is the reparation and indemnity chapter, which is immoral and senseless. There is not a single person among the younger people here who is not unhappy and disappointed at the terms. The only people who approve are the old fire-eaters.'

Letter from one of the British observers at Versailles, Harold Nicolson, 8 June 1919.

SOURCE E

'Yielding to overpowering might, the government of the German Republic declares itself ready to accept and sign the peace treaty. But in so doing, the government of the German Republic in no way abandons its conviction that these conditions of peace are unjust.'

The German government reluctantly accepts the treaty, 1919.

SOURCE F

'I claim that this treaty will be a lighthouse in the deep, warning nations and the rulers of nations against the perils against which Germany shattered itself.'

Lloyd George in the House of Commons, 21 July 1919.

SOURCE G

'Vengeance! German nation! Today in the Hall of Mirrors the disgraceful treaty is being signed. Do not forget it. The German people will with unceasing labour press forward to reconquer the place among nations to which it is entitled. Then will come vengeance for the shame of 1919.'

The reaction of a German newspaper, 28 June 1919.

SOURCE H

'I believe that the campaign for securing out of Germany the general costs of the War was one of the most serious acts of political unwisdom for which our statesmen have been responsible.'

The view of the British economist J. M. Keynes, 1920.

SOURCE I

Protest in Munich against the treaty. ▶

EXERCISE

1 What connection can you see between Sources A, C and F? Explain your answer.

2 What connection can you see between Sources B, E and G? Explain your answer.

3 What connection can you see between Sources D and H? Explain your answer.

4 a Do you think Source G is biased? Give reasons for your answer.
  b Do you think historians will find Source G a useful source? Explain your answer.

5 On the evidence of these sources, do you think the following statements are true or false? In each case explain your answer.
  a All British people thought the peace with Germany was a good one.
  b All Germans felt that the peace treaty was unfair.

1.3 EARLY PROBLEMS OF THE REPUBLIC, 1919–23

The Weimar Republic was severely tested in its first five years, and its very existence was threatened by major problems.

Political problems

Many Germans hated the Republic because they felt that Germany had been betrayed at the end of the First World War. Extreme right-wing groups argued that Germany had not been defeated by the Allies but had been 'stabbed in the back' at home. Some of them therefore tried to overthrow the Republic by means of revolt. These revolts were called *putsches*.

The first was the **Kapp *Putsch***. In 1920 Dr Wolfgang Kapp marched on Berlin with 5,000 supporters, intending to set up a right-wing government. The true government withdrew from Berlin to Dresden. It called on all German workers to refuse to co-operate with Kapp by joining a general strike (see Source A). All essential services stopped immediately – gas, water, electricity and transport. Kapp found that he could not govern Germany in the midst of this chaos. He therefore gave up and fled.

Another *putsch* occurred in 1923 in the Bavarian capital, Munich. This was led by **Adolf Hitler**, who also intended to march on Berlin and seize power. The **Munich *Putsch***, however, was put down by the police. (See pages 12–3).

Violence and murders

Not only the government was threatened. Individuals who carried out its policies also became the targets of extremists. One victim was **Matthias Erzberger**. He had carried out the unpleasant but necessary task of signing the surrender of Germany in 1918, which made him a marked man. In 1921 he was shot and killed while walking in the Black Forest. Another victim was **Walther Rathenau**, the Foreign Minister, who was machine-gunned in a Berlin street.

SOURCE A

'Workers, comrades! The military *putsch* is under way. We refuse to bow to this military pressure. Use every means to prevent the return of bloody reaction. Strike, stop working, strangle this military dictatorship, fight! Not a hand must move, not a single worker must help the military dictatorship! General strike all along the line! Workers, unite!'

The government's appeal to the workers against Kapp, 1920.

SOURCE B

◀ *French troops in the Ruhr, 1923.*

The worthlessness of German banknotes in 1923.

Economic crisis

The economic crisis built up slowly from 1919 and, by 1923, developed into one of the worst bouts of **inflation** ever known. Why did it happen?

By 1918 Germany was bankrupt and exhausted. The Allies, however, did not take this into account. In fact, they made things worse by imposing a severe peace settlement which slowed down Germany's recovery. Then in 1921 Germany was suddenly faced with a **reparations** bill for 136,000 million marks, to be paid in instalments. The German government hoped to reduce the size of these payments, but the other countries, especially France, were not sympathetic. They needed money themselves so that they could pay off their war debts to the United States.

The German government struggled on until 1923, but during that year failed to pay France and Belgium all that was due to them. The French decided to use this as an opportunity to teach the Germans a lesson and sent troops into the **Ruhr**, the most industrialized part of Germany (Source B). The inhabitants of the Ruhr refused to co-operate with the French, who had to bring in their own workers to run essential industries and the railways.

The value of the German mark now fell rapidly, and inflation resulted. Paper money poured off the presses from 300 paper mills and 2,000 printing shops. Even then there were too few banknotes available, so that they had to be overstamped with new values. For example, a 100 mark note might be changed overnight into a million mark note. When compared with other currencies, the mark became completely worthless. In 1919 there were 8.9 marks to the US dollar. By November 1923 the same dollar was worth 4,200 million marks. Sources C and D give an impression of what this inflation meant to the average German.

A situation like this could not last indefinitely. In September 1923 a new Chancellor was appointed, Gustav Stresemann. In November he cancelled the old devalued mark and called in all the notes. He then issued a new currency called the **Rentenmark**. This measure introduced a period of recovery, but many people had been ruined.

'There were extraordinary scenes. A woman who came to her butcher shop with a basketful of marks left them on the pavement as she followed the queue inside to get her meat. On her return she found her marks dumped into the gutter and the basket stolen. On street-car rides the conductor did not accept fares until the end of the ride because the value of the mark would change in a matter of minutes. Housewives had to shop several times a day because a pound of butter might rise five times in cost within 24 hours. Workers had to exchange six weeks' pay (carted in wheelbarrows) for a pair of shoes.

Description by a modern historian of what inflation meant.

1.4 HITLER AND THE NAZI PARTY TO 1923

The first three units have dealt with the special problems facing the new Republic after the First World War. Now we turn our attention to the man who was eventually to destroy this Republic, **Adolf Hitler**.

Hitler's early life to 1919

Hitler was born in Austria in 1889. He left school at 16 and two years later tried to gain admission to the Vienna Academy of Fine Arts. He was considered to lack the necessary talent. Between 1909 and 1914 he lived rough in Vienna, trying to earn a living by painting and selling postcards. At this stage, he was little more than a tramp.

Then, at the beginning of the First World War, his life changed. He joined the German army and served as a corporal on the Western Front. He was wounded and won several decorations, including the Iron Cross. Hitler believed passionately in Germany's cause and was devastated by the German surrender in November 1918; he was certain that the German Army could not have been defeated and that it had been 'stabbed in the back' by the politicians – or 'November criminals' as he called them.

Many other Germans thought along similar lines, and several extreme right-wing parties sprang up. One of these was the **German Workers' Party (DAP)**, a small organization formed in Munich in 1919 by Anton Drexler. Hitler joined this in the same year.

SOURCE B

'The new movement aimed at providing what the others did not: a racialist movement with a firm social base, a hold over the broad masses, welded together in an iron-hard organization, instilled with blind obedience and inspired by a brutal will, a party of struggle and oblivion.'

Hitler describes how the Nazi movement differs from previous parties in an internal party memorandum of 1922.

SOURCE C

'My critical faculty was swept away. Leaning from the rostrum as if he were trying to impel his inner self into the consciousness of all those thousands, he was holding the masses, and me with them, under an hypnotic spell by the sheer force of his conviction.'

Kurt Ludecke describes the effect of one of Hitler's speeches on himself in 1922.

SOURCE A

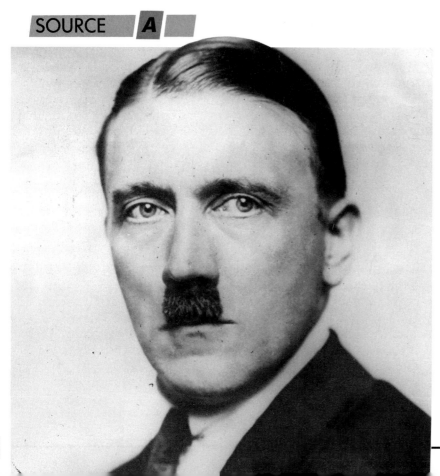

Hitler in 1923.

SOURCE D

Storm-troopers.

SOURCE E

'As a member of the storm troop of the NSDAP, I pledge myself by its storm flag: to be always ready to stake life and limb in the struggle for the aims of the movement; to give absolute military obedience to my military superiors and leaders; to bear myself honourably in and out of service.'

The pledge of the SA, made by all storm-troopers on joining.

Hitler's rise within the party, 1919–22

Drexler soon decided to give Hitler special responsibilities within the DAP. By the end of 1919 Hitler was in charge of propaganda and of developing the party's ideas. In February 1920 Hitler and Drexler drew up the Twenty-Five Point Programme of the German Workers' Party. This stated that the Treaty of Versailles should be scrapped; Germany should expand to include more territory for its people; and Jews were to be deprived of German citizenship. There were also clauses explaining how the DAP intended to change the economy. Finally, the programme demanded the creation of a powerful state authority.

Shortly after this, the party changed its name, at Hitler's suggestion, to the **National Socialist German Workers' Party (NSDAP)**. Its sign was a black swastika in a white circle on a red background. In 1921 Hitler pushed Drexler aside and took over the party leadership himself.

Hitler's strengths

Most of the sources in this unit are intended to show why Hitler rose so quickly to supreme control in the National Socialist ('Nazi') Party. He was convinced that more support would be attracted if the Nazi Party could show itself to be strong in dealing with its opponents. He also believed that parades, banners and marching songs could do as much as political programmes and speeches. In 1921, therefore, he set up the *Sturm Abteilung* (SA) or **storm-troopers** (also known as the Brownshirts). They became involved in numerous street fights, usually against Communists, and broke up rival meetings. Hitler placed a great deal of hope in the SA as he now turned his attention to seizing power.

QUESTIONS

1 Using both the text and the sources, make a list of the qualities Hitler had which might have helped him be a leader of a political party.

2 Which of these qualities do you think was the most important? Give reasons for your answer.

3 In what ways might the storm-troopers have helped the Nazi Party?

1.5 THE MUNICH *PUTSCH*

CAUSATION

During the evening of 8 November 1923 a meeting took place in one of the great beerhalls of Munich. It was addressed by Gustav von Kahr. Suddenly, Hitler burst in, announcing that the hall was surrounded by SA men and that he was taking over the State government of Bavaria. The next stage, he declared, would be a march on Berlin to take over the German government. He tried to obtain the support of Kahr and others by threats. Kahr, however, refused to be intimidated and managed to escape from the hall before the night was out.

Next morning, on 9 November, Hitler tried again. This time he led about 3,000 supporters to the centre of Munich. On the way they were met by about 100 of the Bavarian state police, who had been ordered to disperse the march (Source A). When they opened fire, sixteen Nazis were killed, and the whole *putsch* – or revolt – collapsed. Hitler had kept in the background as the trouble started and managed to escape. But shortly afterwards he was arrested, put on trial for treason and sentenced to five years' imprisonment in Landsberg Castle.

SOURCE B

'In the near future, when we have gained power, we shall have the further duty of taking these creators of ruin, these clouts, these traitors to their state, and hanging them to the gallows to which they belong. Let no one think that in them there has come a change of heart.'

From a speech made by Hitler, 13 April 1923.

SOURCE A

Mounted police about to disperse Hitler's supporters, 9 November 1923.

CAUSATION

SOURCE C

'We wanted to create in Germany the precondition which alone will make it possible for the iron grip of our enemies to be removed from us. We wanted to create order in the state, throw out the drones, take up the fight . . . above all for the highest honourable duty which we, as Germans, know should once more be introduced – the duty of bearing arms. And now I ask you: is what we wanted high treason?'

Hitler's closing speech at his trial, 27 March 1924.

SOURCE D

'When I resume active work, it will be necessary to pursue a new policy. Instead of working to achieve power by an armed coup, we will have to hold our noses and enter the Reichstag against Catholic and Marxist members. If outvoting them takes longer than outshooting them, at least the result will be guaranteed by their own constitution. Sooner or later we shall have a majority, and after that – Germany!'

From a letter written by Hitler while in prison after the failure of the 'putsch'.

SOURCE E

'For us, Parliament is not an end in itself, but simply a means to an end.'

From a speech made by Hitler 10 days after the September 1930 election.

Main reasons for the *putsch*

The most obvious reason is that Hitler wanted to destroy the Weimar Republic. Source B shows clearly that he hated the government. There are, however, more complex reasons which combine with each other, rather like a web. Hitler reasoned that the Republic could be overthrown because it had been weakened by the situation in Germany at the time, especially by the French occupation of the Ruhr and the devastating inflation (see pages 8–9). He also expected to get support from other right-wing leaders who disliked the Republic – including Kahr of Bavaria.

We still need to explain why Hitler conducted his *putsch* in Munich and why he threatened Kahr. One of the reasons why Kahr had been suspicious of the Republic was that he thought it was too soft in dealing with Communism. In 1923, however, the Republic crushed left-wing governments in two states near Bavaria. Kahr now thought that it would be better to wait and see what happened next. Hitler felt his opportunity slipping away and decided to put pressure on Kahr to support his plan to overthrow the Republic. Kahr, as we have seen, refused to be browbeaten and resisted Hitler.

Consequences of the *putsch*

The most immediate result of the *putsch* was Hitler's trial and imprisonment. Again, however, there are more complex factors to consider. For example, during his trial Hitler was given much publicity when he openly attacked the record of the Republic (see Source C). Also, while in prison, he had time to think about the future and organize his ideas more carefully in his book, **Mein Kampf** ('My Struggle').

The long-term result of the Munich *Putsch* was also important. Hitler learned from his mistake and worked out a new way to achieve power. Source D describes what he now intended to do: instead of trying to overthrow the government by a *putsch* he would secure more votes for the Nazis and aim for a majority in the Reichstag. Source E, however, shows his underlying intention. As soon as he gained this majority he would take whatever measures were necessary to destroy the Republic. Time was to show that this new approach would succeed where the old one failed.

EXERCISE

1 What was Hitler's aim when he burst into the beerhall on 8 November 1923?

2 What were the consequences of Hitler's bursting into the beerhall? Give reasons for your answer.

3 Your answers to questions 1 and 2 are different. Does this mean that what people wanted in history is irrelevant? Explain your answer.

4 Was the Munich *putsch* a failure for Hitler and the Nazis? Give reasons for your answer.

1.6 THE STRESEMANN ERA: NAZI FRUSTRATION 1924–9

SOURCE **A**

Gustav Stresemann, Chancellor 1923, Foreign Minister 1923–9.

Between 1924 and the beginning of 1929 Germany recovered from some of its earlier problems and experienced happier times. The Republic seemed much more in control, thanks largely to Foreign Minister **Gustav Stresemann** (Source A). Stresemann was so influential that this is often known as the 'Stresemann era'. During the same period Hitler, who deeply hated the Republic, tried to strengthen the Nazi Party. Yet these were not good years for the Nazis.

Achievements of the Stresemann era

The most important achievements for Germany of this period concerned the economy and foreign policy.

The **economy** recovered quickly from the collapse of the mark and from inflation (see pages 8–9). Part of the reason was the introduction in 1923 of the **Rentenmark** which replaced the old, devalued currency. Germany was also greatly helped by the **Dawes Plan** of 1924. By this the Allies allowed Germany to pay off its reparations in easier stages, reducing what had been a very heavy burden. The **Young Plan** (1929) went further and extended the payments by another fifty-nine years.

SOURCE **B**

'In many respects the League is the heir and executor of the treaties of 1919. Out of these treaties there have arisen in the past many differences between the League and Germany. I hope that our co-operation within the League will make it easier in future to discuss these questions. In this respect mutual confidence will be found a greater creative force than anything else.'

Extract from Stresemann's speech on Germany's entry into the League of Nations, 1926.

Meanwhile, what Germany most needed was money from abroad to get its industries back into production. From 1924 this poured into Germany from the United States in the form of **investment**. The result was spectacular. More goods were produced, and exports rose. As a result, the labour force increased, and unemployment dropped. Most Germans were much better off.

At the same time, Stresemann was also improving Germany's image abroad. In 1925 Germany joined Britain, France, Belgium and Italy in the **Locarno Pact**. By this agreement the five powers promised to keep the existing borders between France, Germany and Belgium. Then in 1926 Stresemann took Germany into the **League of Nations**. This was a courageous move, since many Germans regarded the League as an enemy which would do anything to uphold the Treaty of Versailles. Stresemann intended to show the rest of Europe that Germany was a reformed country and that there was a good case for easing the burdens that had been placed upon it (Source B).

Stresemann died in 1929. This was a major loss to the Republic. He had proved one of the greatest European statesmen of the 1920s.

Hitler refounds the Nazi Party

While Hitler was in prison the Nazi Party fell into disarray. On his release in December 1924 he once again made himself absolute leader. He streamlined the party and divided it into local units called **Gaue** ('districts'), each under a *Gauleiter* appointed by Hitler himself. In 1926 he gained the support of Nazis in northern Germany, particularly Joseph Goebbels, and so extended his control beyond Bavaria. We have seen (pages 12–13) that Hitler was now determined to try to build up a party which would be strong enough to be elected to power in the foreseeable future.

Nazi frustration

Despite these efforts, the Nazis did very badly in three Reichstag elections during the period (Source C). The reason was that the German people were mostly contented during the Stresemann era. What Hitler needed to boost his chances of coming to power legally was for the Republic to face another major crisis.

SOURCE **C**

Date	Nazi seats	Number of larger parties
1924 (May)	16	5
1924 (Dec.)	19	7
1928	17	7

The Nazi Party's performance in Reichstag elections, 1924–8.

1.7 HITLER'S IDEAS

Hitler's ideas are contained in a variety of sources. The most important is *Mein Kampf*, written while Hitler was imprisoned in Landsberg Castle after the Munich *Putsch*. In 1928 he wrote another book. This was not published until 1959 and is usually known as Hitler's *Second Book* or *Secret Book*. We can also work out many of his ideas from his early speeches.

Nationalism and socialism. The party programme, which Hitler drew up in 1920, contained a series of policies which emphasized both nationalism and socialism. **Nationalism** was concerned with reviving Germany's power, expanding Germany's frontiers and 'purifying' the German 'race'. **Socialism** stressed the need to increase state control over the economy. Although the party kept the name 'National Socialist' throughout the period, nationalism was more important than socialism.

Struggle. Underlying all his views on 'racial purity' and German expansion was Hitler's belief that **struggle** was a basic fact of nature (Source A). It made the Nazis particularly ruthless and merciless.

Race. Hitler argued that humans could be subdivided into superior and inferior races. The superior race were the **Aryans**, confined largely to northern Europe, especially Germany. Source B illustrates Hitler's belief that the Aryans had produced all that was worthwhile in human culture. There was a characteristic Aryan appearance (Source C). 'Inferior races' included those of eastern Europe, Asia and Africa. The lowest form of humanity, according to Hitler, was the Jews. He blamed them for all of Germany's misfortunes and regarded them as 'parasites', feeding off the countries in which they lived (Source E). Source D shows how viciously the Nazis portrayed the Jews in their later propaganda.

War and conquest. In *Mein Kampf* and the *Second Book*, Hitler wrote that conquest and expansion were both necessary and natural for a 'healthy' race like the Aryans. Germany was too small for the essential needs of its people. The answer was to gain **'living space'** (*Lebensraum*) at the expense of Poland and Russia. This would involve struggle and war, which would strengthen the Germans for their role as 'master race'. Hitler intended to give priority to this rather than to competing commercially with Britain and the USA (Source F).

Organization and propaganda. After the Munich *Putsch* Hitler tried to increase support for his movement so that it could eventually come to power legally. He made the Nazi Party as efficient as possible and used **propaganda** to spread its appeal. In particular, he smeared the Republic with all kinds of lies.

Leadership. Hitler despised democracy, both within the Nazi Party and at national level. He introduced the *Führer Prinzip* or **'leader principle'**, whereby he would be given total and unquestioning loyalty. He also saw himself as the only true interpreter of what was best for the German people. Policies arrived at as a result of discussion, he insisted, were weak.

SOURCE A

'It has always been the right of the stronger, before God and man, to see his will prevail. All of nature is one great struggle between strength and weakness, an eternal victory of the strong over the weak.'

Hitler's views on struggle, from a speech in 1923.

SOURCE C

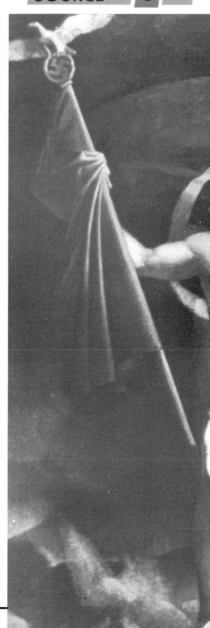

SOURCE B

'All the human culture, all the results of art, science and technology that we see before us today, are almost exclusively the creative product of the Aryan.'

From 'Mein Kampf'.

How Hitler's ideas on race were later applied to the 'ideal' appearance of the Aryan. ▼

SOURCE D

An anti-Jewish poster used to advertise the film 'The Wandering Jew' during the Second World War.

SOURCE E

'Culturally he contaminates art, literature and the theatre, makes a mockery of national feeling, overthrows all concepts of beauty, and instead drags men down into the sphere of his own base nature.'

Hitler's view of 'the Jew'.

SOURCE F

'Germany resolves to change to a clear, far-sighted policy of expansion. It shall thus turn away from all attempts at world trade and international industrial enterprise, and instead concentrate all its forces on providing our nation with sufficient living space. Such space can only be in the east.'

Hitler describing the future expansion of Germany, the 'Second Book', 1928.

1.8 THE DEPRESSION AND HITLER'S SUCCESS, 1929–33

CHANGE

At the beginning of 1929 Hitler was the leader of the seventh largest party in the Reichstag, with little chance of coming to power. Four years later, in January 1933, he was summoned by President Hindenburg and made Chancellor. By this time the Nazis had more seats in the Reichstag than any other party.

This unit explains why the situation was so transformed during these years. We saw on pages 14–15 that Hitler stood little chance when Germany was stable and prosperous. What made the difference was the **Great Depression** which created an economic crisis, boosted support for the Nazis and destroyed the political stability of the Stresemann era.

The German economy and the Depression
In 1919 Germany was badly affected by a worldwide depression which was sparked off by the **Wall Street Crash** in the United States. Almost all US investments in Germany were withdrawn. This was especially serious because German industrial growth after 1924 had depended on foreign loans. As a result many industrialists went bankrupt or had to reduce production. This meant that large parts of the workforce were laid off, and unemployment soared.

Economic crisis led to **social misery**. Many middle- and working-class families were ruined. Some people had to give up their homes because they could no longer afford the rent. Instead, they had to move to makeshift shanty towns. The city streets were filled with men who had no work and no hope. Sources B and C give some impression of their suffering. In this sort of atmosphere the Republic became more and more unpopular since it appeared unable to do anything.

Nazi Party support and the Depression
If you look at Source E you can see a major change in the performance of the various parties in the Reichstag elections. The Nazis gained support at the expense of the National Party, the People's Party and the Democrats. What seems to have happened is that a large number of middle-class voters were so disillusioned as a result of the Depression that they abandoned their usual voting habits and switched to the Nazis. The working class also provided some support for Hitler, although most remained loyal to their traditional party, the Social Democrats, or voted Communist.

Hitler was ready for an economic crisis and did all he could to attract new supporters. He campaigned all over Germany in the elections of 1930 and 1932, frequently addressing several meetings a day. He attracted huge crowds with his attacks on the Republic's economic record and foreign policy.

Hitler's personal fortunes
Despite all this, Hitler was still not strong enough to win power directly. He did not have a majority in the Reichstag and he failed to beat Hindenburg in the 1932 presidential election. In normal times Germany's democracy might have been strong enough to keep Hitler out of power.

SOURCE A

Year	Number unemployed
1928	1,862,000
1929	2,850,000
1930	3,217,000
1931	4,886,000
1932	6,042,000

Unemployment in Germany, 1928–32.

SOURCE B

Effects of the Great Depression.

EXERCISE

1 Which of Sources A to F show change actually taking place?

2 a Which of Sources A to F show the actual result of changes?

  b How reliable would these sources be?

3 Describe the connection between Sources A, B and C.

CHANGE

'No one knew how many there were of them. They completely filled the streets. They stood or lay about in the streets as if they had taken root there. They sat or lay on the pavements or in the roadway and gravely shared out scraps of newspapers among themselves.'

Description of the suffering in Karlshafen (extract from a short story).

The Depression, however, helped Hitler by undermining this democracy. You will remember that the Republic was governed by coalitions because of the nature of the voting system (see page 5). The economic crisis caused the coalition under Müller to fall apart in 1930, as the various members could not agree on what policies to introduce. The next three Chancellors – Brüning, Papen and Schleicher – relied on the President's powers, by article 48 of the constitution, to rule by decree without the support of the Reichstag. In this undemocratic atmosphere Hitler was able to come to power through the back door. In January 1933 Papen wanted to bring down his rival, Schleicher. He persuaded the President to appoint Hitler Chancellor, with Papen as Vice-Chancellor. He even argued that power would moderate Hitler's policies (Source F). Time was to show how wrong Papen was.

A crowd listening to Hitler speaking in Berlin in 1932.

4 Consider the following statements. In each case say whether you think they are true or not and support your answer with details from the text or the sources.
  a Hitler came to power entirely through his own efforts.
  b Hitler made steady progress to power after his release from gaol in 1924.

	1928	1930	1932 July	1932 Nov.
Nazis	13	107	230	196
National Party	79	41	40	51
People's Party	45	30	7	11
Centre	61	68	75	70
Democrats	25	14	4	2
Social Democrats	152	143	133	121
Communists	54	77	89	100

Number of Reichstag seats won by the main parties, 1928–32.

'We believed Hitler when he said that once he was in a position of power and responsibility, he would steer his movement into more ordered channels.'

Papen explaining why Hitler was given a chance in January 1932.

1.9 PEOPLE'S VIEWS OF HITLER BEFORE 1933

EMPATHY

Part One has dealt with the Weimar Republic and Hitler's rise to power. We can now end it by seeing what people at the time thought of events. This is an exercise in 'empathy', which means understanding things from the viewpoints of other people.

The working class   The German working class was divided about what it thought of Hitler. Some had always supported the Nazis, who had, after all, started out as the 'German Workers' Party'. Others were won over as a result of the Depression and unemployment, perhaps encouraged by posters like Source A. On the other hand, most trade union members distrusted the Nazis and remained loyal to the Social Democrats; they might well have been convinced by Source B. Some of the more radical workers switched to the Communists in preference to the Nazis.

The middle class   The German middle class consisted of professional people, including lawyers, civil servants and teachers, together with small shop-keepers and farmers. Usually members of the middle class were moderate and supported the Democrats and the People's Party. In 1929, however, they were badly affected by the Depression. Many went over to the Nazis, convinced that only they knew how to cure Germany's economic problems and attracted by Hitler's attacks on communism. Yet, despite the Depression, many of the middle class refused on principle to vote for Hitler, disliking his ideas and methods.

Big business   Hitler seemed to offer something to everybody. The great industrialists felt that the Nazis were the best guarantee against a Communist revolution which they feared might come about as a result of the Depression. From 1929 onwards they therefore contributed to the funds of the Nazi Party. All the same, they tended to see the Nazis as rather uncivilized and they preferred the more traditional National Party. The problem was that this seemed to be growing weaker.

Nationalists   Most ardent nationalists supported Hitler, since he offered the most drastic methods of destroying the Treaty of Versailles. Some, however, were put off by his views on race (see page 16) which they felt were not an essential part of Germany's interests.

Youth   Young people were often in a difficult position. Some were influenced by their parents; others might be in conflict with them. At school their different loyalties would frequently clash, as Source C shows. What most attracted some young people to the Nazi movement were the parades, banners and feeling of power. But there must also have been a considerable amount of bullying and intimidation.

Women   The right-wing parties in Germany were supported more heavily by women than by men. At first this did not apply to the Nazis, who had rigid views about the role of women as mothers and housewives. Any woman who intended to make a career for herself would find the Nazis acting very much against her interests. Gradually, however, Nazi propaganda began to win female support.

SOURCE **A**

'We want work and bread!' Nazi election poster, 1932.

SOURCE **B**

Social Democratic poster showing what the Nazi Party really meant to the worker, 1932.

EMPATHY

'Leaflets have recently been distributed in the playgrounds of the schools of the city of Oldenburg and its vicinity inviting people to join a National Socialist Pupils' Association.

'A number of pupils have already followed the appeal to join this association. They consider themselves pledged to bully those who disagree with them. In the playground these pupils join together and sing National Socialist combat songs. Children of Republicans are called names, their satchels are smeared with swastikas, and they are given leaflets with swastikas or "Heil Hitler" or "Germany Awake" written on them. In the school in Metjendorf the son of a Republican was beaten up during the break by members of the Pupils' Association so badly that he had to stay at home for a week.'

Complaint about the behaviour of pro-Nazi pupils in schools, 1930.

SOURCE **D**

Nazi poster, 1932. It reads: Women! Millions of men out of work. Millions of children without a future. Save our German families. Vote for Adolf Hitler!

EXERCISE

As you answer the following questions, try to see issues from different points of view. You may wish to refer to the text and sources of other units in Part One.

1 If, in 1932, a teacher had been asked by a young Nazi supporter if he might marry the teacher's daughter, how do you think the teacher would have responded? Explain your answer.

2 How do you think the parents of one of the members of the National Socialist Pupils' Association would have reacted if the school had complained of behaviour such as that described in Source C?

3 a How do you think a working-class German would react to Source A?

  b How do you think a middle-class German would react to Source A?

4 What do you think the people responsible for Source B were trying to do?

5 How do you think German women would feel about the Nazis after seeing Source D?

2.1 HITLER BECOMES DICTATOR, 1933

CHANGE

Hitler's powers increased greatly betweeen 1933 and 1934. He gradually built up his position through four main changes to the German constitution, each following on from the one before.

Hitler gains a majority in the Reichstag

Hitler had been made Chancellor in January 1933 but was still very much under the influence of **President Hindenburg**. There were also only three Nazis in the government, and Hitler had no overall majority in the Reichstag.

Hitler's immediate aim was to achieve such a majority, so that he could get the laws he wanted passed without interference. He therefore called for another election. To make sure that the Nazis won as many votes as possible he persuaded President Hindenburg to declare a state of emergency. The excuse for this was the **Reichstag fire** (see page 24) which was blamed on the Communists. The Nazis also prevented the other parties from putting across their ideas properly, so that Hitler had a strong advantage.

Even with the help of the emergency laws the Nazis still did not manage to gain 50 per cent of the votes, as the results of the election in 1933 show (see diagram below). Although he did have the support of the Nationalists, Hitler needed a two-thirds majority in the Reichstag to introduce the changes he had in mind. To achieve these changes he did two things. First, he made a deal with the Centre Party to secure its co-operation. Second, he used the emergency laws to ban the Communists from taking up the seats they had won in the election.

Hitler takes the power to make laws

The Nazis now used this two-thirds majority to introduce an **Enabling Act** (see Source A). This made it possible for Hitler to make laws for four years without the consent of the Reichstag. It was passed by 444 votes to 94. Only the Social Democrats risked the intimidation of the SA and SS (see page 28) to vote against.

Hitler bans all opposition

Hitler now made sure that there would be no future obstacles to the Nazi dictatorship. In July 1933 all political parties except the Nazis were officially banned (see Source B).

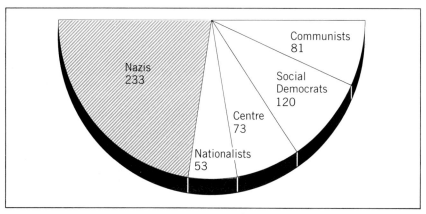

Number of seats won in the Reichstag election of March 1933.

SOURCE A

'The Reichstag has passed the following law. The requirements of legal constitutional change having been met, it is being proclaimed herewith:

Article 1
In addition to the procedure outlined for the passage of legislation in the constitution, the government is also able to pass laws.

Article 3
The laws passed by the government shall be issued by the Chancellor and published in the official gazette.'

The Enabling Act, March 1933.

SOURCE B

'The government has passed the following law, which is being proclaimed herewith:

Article 1
The sole political party existing in Germany is the National Socialist German Workers' Party.'

Law against the New Formation of Parties, July 1933.

SOURCE C

'I swear before God to give my unconditional obedience to Adolf Hitler, Führer of the Reich and of the German people, and I pledge my word as a brave soldier to observe this oath always, even at the peril of my life.'

The army's oath of allegiance to Hitler.

SOURCE **D**

The Reichstag chamber before the fire of 1933.

Hitler becomes Führer

The one person who could still stop Hitler was Hindenburg. The President was old and senile, and his death could be expected shortly. As soon as this happened Hitler hoped to replace him. To do this he needed the support of the army. The army leaders, however, were deeply suspicious of Hitler's SA. In order to reduce their fears and to guarantee the army's help, Hitler later had the leaders of the SA killed in the **Night of the Long Knives** (see page 26–7).

Hitler succeeded in his aim. When Hindenburg died in 1934 Hitler was able to add the powers of President to those he already possessed as Chancellor. He also assumed a new title – Führer – and received an oath of personal allegiance from the army (Source C).

SOURCE  **E**

The Reichstag after Hitler's changes: Hitler speaking in 1939.

EXERCISE

1 Which powers did Hitler have in 1934 that he had not had at the beginning of 1933?

2 Explain how Source A makes Source B possible.

3 What is the importance of Source C?

4 Study Sources D and E.
   a What are the differences?
   b Do these two sources show the changes that took place in Germany between 1933 and 1939? Explain your answer.

2.2 THE REICHSTAG FIRE

EVIDENCE

On the evening of 27 February 1933 Goebbels was entertaining Hitler to dinner. They were distracted by flames in the sky, and from the balcony they saw that the Reichstag building was on fire. In the building itself a Dutchman by the name of Marinus Van der Lubbe was caught with matches and firelighters in his possession. He confessed to the act and was put on trial along with four others. They were accused of being part of a Communist conspiracy.

The Nazis would have found such a plot very useful because they were looking for an excuse to ask President Hindenburg to declare a state of emergency. This, in turn, would help the Nazis in the Reichstag election of March 1933 (see page 22). The Communists were not slow to see this danger. An organization based in Paris claimed that the Nazis started the fire themselves, using Van der Lubbe as a tool.

Van der Lubbe himself denied that he was part of a conspiracy. The court decided to acquit those accused with him, but van der Lubbe was found guilty and executed.

There has always been a great deal of controversy about this incident. In this unit we review the arguments put forward in the primary and secondary sources.

SOURCE **A**

The Reichstag on fire.

SOURCE **B**

How the Nazis interpreted the fire (from the cover of a book called 'Armed Uprising').

EVIDENCE

SOURCE C

'In view of the ever-growing anti-Fascist feeling among the workers, Hitler's election prospects were not good. The disillusionment of the masses would show itself on 5 March in an increased Communist vote. It became necessary to change the situation by some act of provocation. Then the elections could be carried out when violent feeling against the Communists and Socialists was at its height.'

Accusation by the Communist International propaganda organization.

SOURCE E

'I can only repeat that I set fire to the Reichstag all by myself.'

Van der Lubbe's statement at his trial.

SOURCE F

'Actually, it appears certain the Nazis themselves had used an underground passage leading to the Reichstag building to fire it, and used the Dutchman as a cover-up.'

The view of historian T. L. Jarman in the 1950s.

SOURCE G

'Latest evidence tends to acquit the Nazis of this particular crime.'

A more recent opinion, from W. Laqueur.

SOURCE D

Van der Lubbe on trial in Berlin.

EXERCISE

1 Do you think historians trying to explain who was responsible for the Reichstag fire will find Source A a useful source?

2 Do you think Source B might be biased? Give reasons for your answer.

3 Do you think historians will find Source B a useful source? Explain your answer.

4 Were the authors of Source C for or against Hitler? Give reasons for your answer.

5 Do you think Sources F and G help us decide who set fire to the Reichstag?

6 Do the sources here give you enough evidence to suggest who set fire to the Reichstag?

7 Historians clearly disagree about who was responsible for the Reichstag fire. Why do you think this might be?

2.3 NIGHT OF THE LONG KNIVES

CAUSATION

On the night of 30 June and 1 July 1934, **Ernst Röhm** and other SA (storm-troopers') leaders were seized, thrown into various cells and cellars and then shot. The total casualty list was several hundred. The executions were conducted, on the orders of Hitler, by SS firing squads, working at fifteen-minute intervals.

Why did Hitler order the murder of the SA leaders?
The simple explanation for these murders is that Hitler no longer trusted the SA leaders. But we need to examine what lay behind this distrust and see how the various points fit together.

In the first place, the SA had an extremely bad reputation, as Source B shows, and this worried Hitler increasingly. Second, we know that Röhm wanted to push Hitler into certain policies which Hitler thought unwise (Sources C and D). Hitler was concerned that the SA leaders' self-assertiveness would force the army to protect itself – and that might mean the army overthrowing the Nazi regime. He later explained his worries about Röhm in a speech to the Reichstag (Source E). This was *after* the murders had taken place.

So far Hitler's motive seems clear. Now we come across some complications. In the first place, the Nazi party had always stressed that the SA and German army were close partners. The letter written by Hitler to Röhm only five months before the murders (Source F) could not have been friendlier.

 SOURCE B

'The SA contained a very high proportion of thugs and social outcasts. Many were men with a criminal record, thieves and even murderers.'

The type of men who joined the SA.

 SOURCE C

'I regard the Reichswehr now only as a training school for the German people. The conduct of war, and therefore of mobilization as well, in future is the task of the SA.'

From a letter from Röhm to Hitler.

 SOURCE D

'The generals are a lot of old fogeys. They never have a new idea. I'm the nucleus of the new army, don't you see.'

In conversation, Röhm gives his views to a friend.

 SOURCE A

Ernst Röhm, eliminated in the Night of the Long Knives.

 SOURCE E

'After the month of May, there could be no further doubt that the Chief of Staff, Röhm, was busied with ambitious schemes which, if realized, could only lead to the most violent disturbances.'

From Hitler's speech to the Reichstag, 13 July 1934.

CAUSATION

SOURCE F

'I feel compelled to thank you, my dear Ernst Röhm, for the imperishable services which you have rendered to the National Socialist movement and the German people, and to assure you how very grateful I am to call such men as you my friends and fellow-combatants.'

From a letter from Hitler to Röhm, 1 January 1934.

SOURCE G

'If Hitler was to secure their support for his succession to the Presidency, the Army . . . in return were determined to exact the removal of the SA threat to take over the Army.'

From A. Bullock, 'Hitler: A Study in Tyranny'.

SOURCE H

'It is not likely that the swift disintegration of the Nazi regime will be checked as a result of the spectacular crushing this weekend of the mysterious revolt of the Brown Army leaders. Nazism is discredited among large sections of the German people.'

'News Chronicle', 2 July 1934.

How can we explain these inconsistencies? One solution is that Röhm misled Hitler about his intentions. This is certainly what Hitler later argued and it gave him the excuse to take drastic action. A more complicated reason is given by the historian Alan Bullock (Source G). Bullock argues that Hitler hoped to succeed Hindenburg as President. He needed the support of the army, and the army wanted the removal of the threat from the SA. Hitler could have used the SA to destroy any possible threat to him from the army, but this would only have made him totally dependent on the SA in the future, something he wanted very much to avoid. He could, however, manage the army more easily if he had to. This all meant that the SA and not the army was to be his target.

The results of the murders

Hitler's position was greatly strengthened by the murders. The army supported him when Hindenburg died, helped him become President and swore an oath of allegiance to him. Yet it did not seem simple at the time. A British newspaper believed that the murders were the last desperate attempt to prevent Hitler falling from power (Source H). Although time has shown this analysis to have been wrong, we should not forget how difficult it is to see results clearly straight after an event.

We should also not assume that the consequence remained the same for a long time afterwards. We know that Hitler continued to benefit, but the German army did not. The powers of the army were steadily reduced, and Hitler completely reorganized the Reichswehr into a new army, the **Wehrmacht**, more directly under his control.

Finally, what of the consequences for the SA storm-troopers? The Brownshirts never again played an important part in key decisions, and their security role was taken over completely by the SS. Yet it was the leadership which had been destroyed in the night of the Long Knives, not the SA itself, which continued to play a role in mass rallies and demonstrations.

EXERCISE

1 What advantages were there for Hitler in having the SA crushed? Explain your answer.

2 Do you think the condition of Hindenburg's health can have been a cause for the Night of the Long Knives? Explain your answer.

3 Source B suggests that a dislike of the reputation of many SA leaders may have been a cause of the Night of

the Long Knives. Do you think that this is likely? Give reasons for your answer.

4 The German army did not do any of the killing. Does this mean it had no part in causing the massacre? Give reasons for your answer.

5 Why do you think Hitler ordered the destruction of the SA? Explain your answer.

2.4 THE NAZI POLICE STATE

Nazi Germany is often described as a **totalitarian** state. This means that the individual was completely under the power of those in authority. One of the most important ways of maintaining power and control was to set up a security system which could make sure that Nazi ideas and policies were enforced and wipe out any opposition. The two organizations responsible for this task were the **SS** and the **Gestapo**.

The SS

The SS was a military corps set up in 1925. In its early days it was part of the SA, although distinguishable from it because its members wore black rather than brown shirts. It was intended to be a small and highly disciplined group, in contrast to the unreliable thugs of the SA. In 1929 it came under the control of **Heinrich Himmler**, who used it to put into practice the racial policies of the Nazi Party (Source B). In 1934 the SS played an important part in wiping out the leadership of the SA (see pages 26–7), and from this date it replaced the SA as the most important security force in Germany. In 1936 it took over the police force, including the Gestapo.

The SS has been called a 'state within a state'. It had its own schools and factories, even race farms which were set up to produce 'perfect' German children. Eventually the SS consisted of three main sections. One was responsible for security. Another was the **Waffen SS**, the most committed and dependable units within the armed forces. The third was the 'death's head units'; during the Second World War these manned the concentration camps and were responsible for carrying out the extermination of the Jews (see pages 58–9).

The Gestapo

Gestapo is the abbreviation of *Geheime Staatspolizei* (Secret State Police). The Gestapo was set up by **Hermann Goering** in 1933. In 1936, as we have seen, it was linked to the SS and came under the supervision of **Reynhard Heydrich**, one of the most ruthless and feared of all the Nazis. Himmler was Heydrich's superior, but in

SOURCE C

'Any attempt to gain recognition for, or even uphold, different ideas will be ruthlessly dealt with as the symptom of an illness which threatens the healthy unity of the state. To discover the enemies of the state, watch them and render them harmless at the right moment is the duty of a political police. In order to fulfil this duty, the political police must be free to use every means suited to achieve the desired end.'

The political purpose of the Gestapo, according to deputy chief of the Gestapo, Werner Best.

SOURCE D

Death sentences for 'political oppression',
    1930–2:   8
    1934–9:   534

Number under 'protective arrest',
    1939: 162,734

Numbers in concentration camps, 1939:

Dachau	4,000
Mauthausen	1,500
Sachsenhausen	6,500
Buchenwald	5,300
Flossenburg	1,600
Ravensbruck	2,500

SOURCE A

'The basis for interpreting all legal sources is the National Socialist philosophy, especially as expressed in the party programme, and in the utterances of our Führer.'

SOURCE B

'I have had one unalterable aim in mind for the eleven years in which I have been Reichsführer SS: to create an Order of Pure Blood for the service of Germany. This Order will go into action with unshakeable determination without sparing itself.'

Hans Frank's definition of justice, 1936.

The purpose of the SS, according to Himmler in 1940.

Statistics of victims of the police state before 1940.

Prisoners in Dachau.

practice the two co-operated closely. The main purpose of the Gestapo is shown in Source C. Heydrich's deputy, Werner Best, made sure that any opposition was dealt with by the most ruthless measures.

Effect on the German people

Most Germans never came into direct contact with the SS or Gestapo because they never questioned Hitler's authority or policies. Those who were brave enough to challenge the system were liable to arrest – often late at night – and questioning under torture. Punishments included internment in a concentration camp or execution.

Source E shows some prisoners in Dachau concentration camp. Their individuality seems to have been wiped out, but these faces perhaps belong to intellectuals, dissidents or political opponents. There might also be several Jews among them, although it was not until after 1941 that the camps were filled with Jews sent for extermination by the SS.

The law did nothing to protect the individual from the activities of the SS and Gestapo. In a democracy there would be limits set by the law on the government and police and upheld in the courts. This was not, however, the case in Nazi Germany. Source A shows the opinion of Hans Frank, who was in charge of justice: the law was, in practice, 'Nazified'. Many judges were appointed for their loyalty to the Nazi Party and were therefore unlikely to be concerned about individual rights. A good example was Judge Roland Freisler, who ranted and screamed at the defendants in his court. Source F shows him in action at a famous trial in 1944.

▼ *Judge Freisler presiding over a treason trial in 1944.*

2.5 CONTROLLING THE MINDS OF THE PEOPLE

We saw on pages 28–9 that terror was one way in which a totalitarian state could be upheld. Another was by the control of all forms of expression and communication. This was done by **propaganda** and **censorship**. In overall control of this was Goebbels, who headed the Nazi **Ministry of People's Enlightenment and Propaganda**, set up in 1933.

Use of radio There were more radios per head of population in Germany than in any other country in Europe. Both Hitler and Goebbels realized the importance of this form of communication at the outset and encouraged people to use it (Source A). Hitler made numerous broadcasts which would have been listened to by workforces in industry, pupils in the classroom and families at home.

SOURCE A

SOURCE B

'The art of propaganda lies in understanding the emotional ideas of the great masses and finding, through a psychologically correct form, the way to the attention and thence to the heart of the broad masses.'

Hitler on propaganda.

SOURCE C

'I hereby expel you from the National Chamber of Fine Arts and forbid you, effective immediately, any activity – professional or amateur – in the field of graphic arts.'

From a government official's letter to a German artist.

SOURCE D

◀ *Nazi poster showing the importance of radio. The caption reads: 'All of Germany listens to the Führer on national radio.'*

SOURCE E

'A roadsweeper sweeps a thousand microbes into the gutter with one brushstroke; a scientist preens himself on discovering a single microbe in the whole of his life.'

The Minister of Education commenting on scientific research in universities.

SOURCE F

'In the next issue there must be a lead article, featured as prominently as possible, in which the decision of the Führer, no matter what it will be, will be discussed as the only correct one for Germany.'

Official instruction to the press, 1 September 1939.

▲ *How the Nazis saw the role of women.*

Control of the arts   Literature was affected by censorship on a massive scale. The works of over 2,500 writers were officially banned. Nazi officials and storm-troopers ransacked public and university libraries and burned millions of books on huge bonfires. **Music** was also carefully scrutinized. Mendelssohn was removed from the list of composers whose works could be played, because he was partly Jewish. Instead, a special place was given to the operas of Richard Wagner. Hitler greatly admired these because they dealt with heroic German legends from the past. **Art** was also censored. Source C is taken from a letter from a government official informing an artist that his work has been judged 'degenerate'. This painter had 608 of his works seized, some of which were displayed in a special exhibition of 'degenerate' art in Munich. The same exhibition also showed a number of paintings by famous artists, including Picasso. The Nazis disapproved of most forms of modern art.

Control of the universities   In most countries universities play an important part in scientific research. In Nazi Germany, however, the government interfered with this research. The Nazi leaders sometimes showed a complete misunderstanding of its importance, as Source E illustrates. Several physicists fled from Germany during the 1930s, the most notable of whom was Albert Einstein.

The control of the press   The Germans were enthusiastic newspaper readers. The Nazis continued to encourage this but made sure that all news came from officially approved agencies. Journalists were directed by the press department of the Ministry of People's Enlightenment and Propaganda and were given regular briefings on what line to take in their articles. Source F shows how far the Nazis were prepared to go in ensuring that Hitler received the best possible coverage.

Rallies   The Nazis continued to show their love of mass rallies and displays, the most spectacular of which were held in **Nuremberg**. Hitler also used the **1936 Olympic Games** in Berlin for propaganda purposes – glorifying Nazi rule – and attempting to demonstrate to the rest of the world the physical 'superiority' of the 'master race'. This was only partly successful. Although Germany headed the medals table at the end of the games, several key track events had been won by the black United States athlete **Jesse Owens**.

The role of women   During the Weimar Republic, women had gradually been given more opportunities, and many had taken up careers. The Nazis frowned on this since they had a fixed idea of women's role in society (Source D). A lot of pressure was applied to women lawyers and doctors to give up their jobs. Had it been possible, Hitler would have favoured the vast majority of women being forced to stay at home.

2.6 EDUCATION AND YOUTH

EMPATHY

The purpose of this unit is to suggest what it might have been like to be of school age in Hitler's Germany. It concentrates on secondary education and youth movements.

Education

What do you consider to be the main purpose of education? Is it to provide occupational qualifications? Or is there a broader aim? School students in Germany would have been left in no doubt about what the authorities considered most important; look at Source A. Many students may well have accepted this view, but some must have had their doubts.

SOURCE B

Periods	Monday	Tuesday	Wednesday	Thursday	Friday	Saturday
8:00–8:45	Deutsch	Deutsch	Deutsch	Deutsch	Deutsch	Deutsch
8:50–9:35	Geog.	History	Singing	Geog.	History	Singing
9:40–10:25	Race study	Race study	Race study	Ideology	Ideology	Ideology
10:25–11:00	Recess, with sports and special announcements					
11:00–12:05	Domestic science with mathematics, every day					
12:10–12:55	Eugenics – Health Biology, alternating					

Summary of the timetable at a girls' school.

Sources B and C show what type of education was provided for the two sexes. Although there are common subjects, the overall emphasis is very different. The assumption seems to be that all girls should be prepared for motherhood and homecraft, while boys should be steered towards an acceptance of war. Again, this could have been very popular, but there would inevitably have been girls interested in going out to work and boys with no military leanings. What would their lives have been like?

All students would have been indoctrinated with race studies and especially with anti-Jewish propaganda (Source D). Some would have been excited about being considered members of the 'master race' and might have felt a growing hatred towards the Jewish members of their class. But would such feelings have been shared by everyone? Some students might have been sympathetic to the Jews, although they would have hesitated to show this openly.

Youth movements

Outside the classroom the youth of Germany were organized into several movements. Boys between the ages of 6 and 10 were enrolled in the **Pimpf** ('Little Fellows') where they were taught to enjoy exercise, hiking and camping and were also introduced to Hitler's ideas. Between the ages of 10 to 14 they joined the **Deutsche Jungvolk** (German Young People), in which they swore an oath of personal allegiance to Hitler and became more familiar with military discipline and military music (Source E). Finally, between 14 and 18, boys were expected to devote themselves to the **Hitler Jugend** (Hitler Youth), which placed most emphasis on military training along the lines of the SA.

SOURCE A

'The whole purpose of education is to create Nazis.'

Minister of Education.

SOURCE C

'German Language, History, Geography, Chemistry and Mathematics must concentrate on military subjects – the glorification of military service and of German heroes.'

The purpose of education for boys.

SOURCE D

Anti-Jewish studies in the classroom. A drawing in a youth magazine.

SOURCE E

Girls up to the age of 14 belonged to the **Jungmädel** (Young Maidens), in which they were trained for health and motherhood. This was taken further, between the ages of 14 and 21, in the **Bund Deutscher Mädel** (League of German Maidens); Source F gives an account of life in the League.

From Source F we also get an insight into how the members of youth organizations regarded the activities they had to undertake. Of course, not all young people would have enjoyed this type of existence. There might also have been strong parental influences against the movements (Source H).

Some Nazi leaders also considered it important that a certain amount of time should be spent by young people in **cultural activities**. A great favourite was music (Source G).

◀ *The 'Deutsche Jungvolk', for boys aged 10 to 14.*

SOURCE F

'We had to be present at every public meeting and at youth rallies and sports. The weekends were crammed full with outings, campings and marches. It was all fun in a way, and we certainly got plenty of exercise, but it had a bad effect on our school reports. We had no time for homework.'

Description of the League of German Maidens, for girls aged 14 to 21.

SOURCE H

'I think one of the worst effects of the whole Nazi youth movement is that our children no longer get any peace or quiet, and I dread to think the kind of people they will grow up into if they are subject to this incessant thundering of propaganda all the time.'

How a German mother felt. From E. Amy Buller, 'Darkness Over Germany', 1945.

EXERCISE

Use the material in this unit and remember to show a range of attitudes.

1 How would you expect a boy educated in Hitler's Germany to react to the following statements.
  a War is good.
  b A woman's place is in the home.
  c There is no point in learning history.

2 How would you expect a girl educated in Hitler's Germany to react to the following statements:
  a War is good.
  b A woman's place is in the home.
  c There is no point in learning history.

3 Hitler was often described as being very good with children. Do you think this means he was liked by all children in Germany?

4 Why do you think Hitler and the leading Nazis thought education was important?

SOURCE G

◀ *Nazi official and family.*

2.7 THE PERSECUTION OF THE JEWS

CHANGE

The Jews have been among the most persecuted people in history. During the Middle Ages most European countries took away their rights, expelled them or even executed them. This was often out of resentment against their economic success. Source E, for example, shows the burning of Jews in medieval Germany. Later, their conditions gradually improved. Many countries gave Jews full rights during the nineteenth and early twentieth centuries.

During the Weimar Republic, Germany's Jews were considered citizens in every respect. They were to be found in all walks of life, especially in professions such as law, medicine, the universities and the civil service. Then came a terrible reverse. Between 1933 and 1945 the Jews were once again persecuted. By the time that the Third Reich had ended, most of Germany's Jews had been deliberately wiped out, along with millions of others throughout Europe. This twelve-year period represents one of the most horrifying changes in history.

Denial of civil rights, 1933–8

During 1933–8 German Jews were deprived of their rights and the protection of the law. As yet, however, physical violence was not the main method used. From March 1933 Hitler ordered the SA to stand outside Jewish shops, to turn away customers (Source A). In April, Jews were forced to give up their jobs in the civil service, although President Hindenburg made sure that exceptions were made for those who had served in, or lost a member of the family in, the First World War. From September, Jews were not allowed to inherit land.

In 1935, a particularly bad year, Jews were excluded from parks, swimming-baths, restaurants and public buildings. They were also deprived of their citizenship and of the right to vote. The **Nuremberg Laws** banned marriages between Jews and non-Jews (Source B). Throughout the period, Jews were subjected to constant insult in the schools and in the crude newspaper of **Julius Streicher**, *Der Stürmer*, which invented horrible stories and presented them as 'facts' (Source C).

Bad though conditions were, there was still some restraint during this period. In 1936 Hitler actually reduced the persecution to coincide with the increase in the number of foreign visitors attending the Olympic Games in Berlin.

The persecution increases, 1938–41

After the beginning of 1938 the situation deteriorated rapidly. The main reason was that the Nazi leaders had become much more confident and less concerned about what the rest of the world thought about their anti-Jewish policies. Germany was now playing a more active part in Europe and was expanding its frontiers. There seemed to be nothing holding Hitler back from introducing more severe anti-Semitic measures. The last remaining rights of the Jews were taken away. Jews could no longer choose names for their children, except from an approved list, and Jewish doctors had their qualifications cancelled.

SOURCE A

Deutsche!
Wehrt Euch!
Kauft nicht bei Juden!

A storm-trooper organizing the boycott of a Jewish shop, 1933.

SOURCE B

'1 Marriages between Jews and citizens of German or kindred blood are hereby forbidden. Marriages performed despite this ban are void.

'2 Extramarital intercourse between Jews and citizens of German or kindred blood is forbidden.'

From the Nuremberg Laws, 1935.

SOURCE C

'The blood of the victims is to be forcibly tapped . . . the fresh (or powdered) blood of the slaughtered child is further used by young married Jewish couples, by pregnant Jewesses, for circumcision and so forth.'

From Streicher's newspaper, 'Der Stürmer'.

CHANGE

On 9 November 1938 there occurred a series of violent incidents now known as **Kristallnacht** (Crystal Night). Over 7,000 Jewish shops were smashed throughout Germany, and many synagogues were burned down. Up to 40,000 Jews were rounded up and sent to concentration camps. All this was in retaliation for the shooting of a German official in the Paris embassy by a Jew.

The 'final solution', 1941–5

During 1941–5 the Nazis exterminated about six million Jews in camps such as Auschwitz, Treblinka and Sobibor. The decision was taken in 1941, and the **'final solution'** to the 'Jewish problem' was given to Heydrich to direct. Many of the details were supervised by **Adolf Eichmann**. This murderous policy was perhaps at the back of Hitler's mind from the time that he wrote *Mein Kampf*; but it took the special situation of the Second World War to convince him that it could be put into practice. The 'final solution' is dealt with in more detail on pages 58–9.

SOURCE D

'At 3 a.m. on 10 November 1938 was unleashed a barrage of Nazi ferocity as had had no equal hitherto in Germany, or very likely anywhere else in the world since savagery began. Jewish buildings were smashed into and contents demolished or looted, three synagogues in Leipzig were fired simultaneously by incendiary bombs and all sacred objects and records desecrated or destroyed.'

Description of Kristallnacht by the United States consul in Leipzig, 1938.

SOURCE E

Burning of the Jews in medieval Germany, from Schedal's 'Chronicle'.

SOURCE F

'1 Jews over the age of six are forbidden to show themselves in public without a Jew's star.
'2 The Jew's star consists of a six-pointed star of yellow cloth with black borders equivalent in size to the palm of the hand. The inscription is to read 'JEW' in black letters. It is to be sewn to the left breast of the garment, and to be worn visibly.'

Nazi police decree, 1941.

EXERCISE

1 Draw a timeline which shows the events mentioned between 1933 and 1945. Is there a turning-point in the experience of the Jews in Nazi Germany? Explain your answer.

2 Do you think war changed the position of the Jews, or speeded up what was happening anyway? Give reasons for your answer.

3 Does Source E show that there had been no real change in German attitudes towards Jews since the Middle Ages?

4 Historians need to be very careful with the words they use. Do you think there is any difference between 'change' and 'progress'? Give reasons for your answer.

2.8 THE NAZI ECONOMY AND REARMAMENT, 1933–9

Ever since it had become a united country in 1871, Germany had been one of Europe's major military powers. Even so, it had been defeated in the First World War, and the Treaty of Versailles had imposed severe limitations on the number of German troops and armaments (Source A; see also pages 6–7). Hitler was determined to change this and to destroy the Versailles settlement. He wanted to extend the army from 100,00 volunteers to a mass army of conscripts.

How was the economy related to this? For the first three years of Nazi rule (1933–5), there were attempts to prevent rearmament dominating the entire economy. From 1936, however, all restraints were dropped, and under the **Four-Year Plan** the German economy was prepared for war.

The economy, 1933–5

At this stage **Hjalmar Schacht** was in charge of the economy. He aimed to improve Germany's trading position in the world and made a number of trade agreements with less developed countries. By these Germany would import raw materials which would be paid for by industrial goods. In his **New Plan** of 1934, Schacht also tried to control imports into Germany and to strengthen the currency. These were sensible policies, but Hitler felt they were too slow to produce results. He had already started to rearm Germany and now wanted to quicken the pace. Schacht, for his part, felt that a balanced and healthy economy could not be achieved with further rearmament.

SOURCE

'By a date which must not be later than 31 March 1920, the German army must not comprise more than seven divisions of infantry and three divisions of cavalry.'

Article 160 of the Treaty of Versailles, 1919.

SOURCE

'We demand abolition of a mercenary army and formation of a people's army.'

Article 22 of the Nazi Party Programme, 1920.

SOURCE

'The extent of the military development of our resources cannot be too large, nor its pace too swift. If we do not succeed in bringing the German army as rapidly as possible to the rank of premier army in the world, then Germany will be lost!

'I thus set the following tasks: i) The German armed forces must be operational within four years. ii) The German economy must be fit for war within four years.'

From Hitler's memorandum on the Four-Year Plan, 1936.

SOURCE C

◄ *Nazi naval expansion: launching the hull of the 'Admiral Graf Spee' on 30 June 1934.*

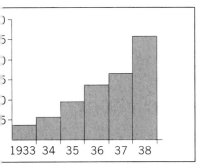

*otal military expenditure of the
erman government, 1933–8.*

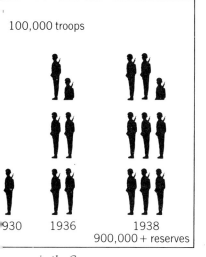

100,000 troops

930   1936   1938
900,000 + reserves

*ncrease in the German army,
930–8.*

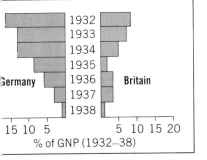

15 10 5   5 10 15 20
% of GNP (1932–38)

*German and British expenditure on
rmament as a percentage of gross
ational product (GNP), 1932–8.*

The Four-Year Plan, 1936–40

In 1936 Hitler imposed his own views. He issued a secret memorandum in which he said that a Four-Year Plan would be introduced. Rearmament would increase rapidly, and Germany would prepare for war. The plan was placed under the control of Goering, who replaced Schacht. **Military expenditure** now rose rapidly, as the armed forces grew.

Another purpose of the Four-Year Plan was to make Germany self-sufficient in essential **raw materials**, largely through home-produced substitutes. This was known as **autarchy**. As a result Germany produced more oil and 460 per cent more plastics.

People like Schacht doubted that Hitler could provide Germans with a better standard of living *and* prepare for war. Yet both of these aims were attempted. Pages 38–41 show that in some ways conditions did improve, although not as much as they could have done. Sacrifices were therefore made for rearmament. On the other hand, this rearmament was not total. By 1939 Germany was ready only for the sort of war which could be won quickly; otherwise the economy would soon be exhausted. Hitler's solution was to defeat his enemies by a sudden blow and then feed off their economies. Pages 54–5 show how he tried to do this through **Blitzkrieg**, or 'lightning war'.

SOURCE   **E**

Artillery works in Düsseldorf, 1939.

2.9 WORK AND LEISURE

Nazi policy on work

As soon as he came to power, Hitler turned his attention to reducing unemployment (see pages 40–1) and making the fullest possible use of the workforce. This was done by reducing people's right to choose the type of job they wanted. Millions were organized into the **RAD** ('National Labour Service') and put to work building **autobahns** (motorways) and public buildings. Source A shows 40,000 workers in the RAD at a Nuremberg rally.

All the Nazi leaders regarded the **trade unions** as a major threat to discipline and obedience. Sources B and C provide evidence of this view. In 1933 free trade unions were banned. This meant an end to the rights taken for granted by workers in free countries: collective bargaining with employers over pay and conditions and, as a last resort, the right to go on strike.

Nazi workers' organizations

The **German Labour Front (DAF)** was set up by the Nazis to replace the free trade unions. Its aim is clearly stated in Source D. It had total control over workers in factories, mines, munition plants and shipyards. It regulated working times (which were several hours longer per week) and set levels of pay (which increased hardly at all). It also had powers to punish workers. The German Labour Front set up two other organizations: Beauty of Labour and Strength through Joy.

Beauty of Labour (Schönheit der Arbeit or SDA) aimed to improve conditions at work such as cleanliness, lighting, noise levels, ventilation and hot meals. The idea was that people would be willing to work extra hours without higher pay because their working conditions would be so much better. They were also persuaded that hard work was a noble and beautiful thing (hence the name of the organization).

SOURCE A

Forty thousand workers being presented to Hitler for inspection.

SOURCE B

'Today we are opening the second chapter of the National Socialist revolution. You may say, You have absolute power: what more do you want? True, we have power, but we do not yet have the whole nation, we do not have you workers 100 per cent; and it is you whom we want. We will not let you alone until you give us your entire and genuine support. You too shall be freed from the last Marxist manacles, so that you may find your way to the people.

'Workers, I swear to you we shall not only preserve everything which exists, we shall build up even further the protection of the worker's rights, so that he can enter the new National Socialist state as a completely worthwhile and respectable member of the nation.'

The Nazi Minister of Labour gives notice of changes to be made in the labour movement; a proclamation of 2 May 1933.

SOURCE C

'The action against the Free Trade Unions corresponds completely with the struggle against Marxism which has been proclaimed by the Führer, Adolf Hitler. The Reich government believes that Marxism must not be allowed to hide behind the trade unions and to continue the struggle in disguise.'

Official statement explaining action against the trade unions, 4 May 1933.

SOURCE D

'The aim of the Labour Front is to educate all Germans who are at work to support the National Socialist state and to indoctrinate them in the National Socialist mentality.'

Proclamation to all working Germans, 27 November 1933.

SOURCE F

Strength through Joy poster.

SOURCE E

Concerts, popular entertainments, operas, operettas, theatre, variety, cabaret, evening variety shows, films, exhibitions, guided tours, basic (sporting) course, special gymnastics, light athletics, swimming, boxing, wrestling, games, water sports, winter sports, special sports, factory sports, vacation journeys, short trips, cruises, hikes.

Leisure-time activities organized by Strength through Joy.

Strength through Joy (Kraft durch Freude, or KDF) was intended to help keep the workforce contented and happy by laying on a wide range of activities to fill people's leisure time. Source F shows a publicity poster reminding workers what was being done for them. The pastimes available are listed in Source E. The most loyal and productive workers could even qualify for a cruise on a Strength through Joy liner. German workers were constantly told that they were far better off than their fellow-workers in the Soviet Union or the West.

2.10 HOW PROSPEROUS WERE PEOPLE UNDER NAZI RULE?

EVIDENCE

This unit concentrates on evidence from two types of source: photographs and statistics. These will be used to check the accuracy of Source A.

Evidence from the photographs

Sources B and C both deal with the less wealthy parts of German society. One shows a rural family, the other the family of an SA man – likely to be from the working class.

One possible way of measuring prosperity is to look at car ownership. The Nazis introduced a new 'people's car', the **Volkswagen**, as shown in Source D. The intention was to give more people the opportunity to possess a car by making the design simple and keeping costs low. We need to look at Source E to see just how many people benefited from this policy. In other words, Source D by itself may be misleading; it needs to be checked against other evidence.

Evidence from statistics

Lists of figures can be an important basic source of information. Yet it is surprising how much we can change our conclusions drawn from them, simply by checking against other statistics. If you examine Sources F to J you will find that each adds more to the one before, to build up a more complete picture. You should then have enough information to agree or disagree with Source A.

SOURCE **A**

'No one who is acquainted with German conditions would suggest that the standard of living is a high one, but the important thing is that it has been rising in recent years.'

How prosperous were the Germans under the Nazis? The view of a Cambridge University economics lecturer in 1938.

SOURCE **B**

A peasant family in East Prussia, 1934. ▲

SOURCE **D**

SOURCE **C**

The family of an SA man, 1937.

SOURCE E

'During the 1930s total car ownership trebled in Germany and doubled in Britain, but even so the pre-war proportion of car ownership was still 50 per cent below the British level of four years earlier.'

Car ownership in Germany and Britain, according to a modern historian.

Ceremonial opening of the Volkswagen factory, 1938. The photograph shows the three 'people's car' models. ▼

SOURCE F

Unemployed in Germany
(in millions)

1928	1.4	1935	2.2
1932	5.6	1936	1.6
1933	4.8	1937	0.9
1934	2.7	1938	0.5

SOURCE G

Index of wages

1928	125	1936	100
1933	88	1938	106
1934	94		

The term 'index' means that the wages in one year, in this case 1936, are taken to be 100, and the other years are measured against this.

SOURCE H

National income
(in thousand millions of marks)

1928	72	1936	64
1932	43	1938	80
1933	44		

'National income' means the total value of goods and services produced.

SOURCE I

Wages as a percentage of national income

1928	62%	1934	62
1932	64	1936	59
1933	63	1938	57

SOURCE J

Index of industrial and consumer goods

Industrial goods		Consumer goods
100	1928	100
56	1933	80
81	1934	91
114	1936	100
144	1938	116

Industrial goods include machinery and armaments; consumer goods are items of everyday household or personal use.

EXERCISE

1 Compare Sources B and C. Do you think one family looks better off than the other? Give reasons for your answer.

2 Does Source D support the view of the German economy given in Source A? Explain your answer.

3 Using the sources here, say whether you think each of the following statements is true or false. In each case give reasons for your answer.
   a There was much less employment after the Nazis came to power.
   b Most Germans were better off after the Nazis came to power.
   c While wages were going up, national income was going down.
   d Because of the increased wages Germany was increasing the production of consumer goods faster than industrial goods.

4 Do you think the judgement about the German economy in Source A is correct? Explain your answer.

5 Do these sources suggest who or what was really benefiting from the growth of the German economy? Explain your answer.

6 Which, if any, of these sources are secondary sources? Give reasons for your answer.

7 How useful are statistics as sources for historians?

2.11 RELIGION IN NAZI GERMANY

Why the churches accepted Hitler in 1933

At a simple level, we could say that the churches came to an agreement with the Nazis because they had no choice. What else could they have done? They could not have prevented Hitler from coming to power and they certainly would not have been able to remove him.

There are, however, other factors, which make up a 'web' of causation. First, the churches were never strong supporters of the Weimar Republic because they felt that it did not do enough to promote religion. Instead, the Republic seemed to them to be concerned with material things. Second, after 1929 the Republic was struggling to survive – so why try to save it? Many people at the time thought that there were two possible alternatives: the Communists and the Nazis. The churches feared communism above everything else, mainly because it was based on *atheism*. The only possibility, therefore, was Nazism.

This brings us to the third factor. Hitler seemed at this stage actually to value Christianity (Source A), and so the churches welcomed him for a positive reason. Catholic leaders believed Hitler would be more effective than the Weimar Republic in providing for *all* the needs of the German people.

Results of the churches' acceptance of Hitler

Source C shows that some Protestant clergy were prepared to allow the display of Nazi uniforms and flags in their churches. In 1933 the Nazi authorities and the Catholic Church signed an agreement known as **the Concordat**. On the surface, then, it appears that there may have been close co-operation between the church and state from 1933 onwards.

But the situation was more complex than this. The Protestants soon discovered that they could not agree on how *much* they should co-operate with the Nazis. Some went the whole way and formed the **German Christian Movement** (Source D), which was, in effect, a Nazi church. Others protested strongly against the new church (Source F). Some individuals, like **Pastor Niemöller**, became active opponents of the Nazis and ended up in concentration camps.

The Catholics also had difficulties. They had accepted Hitler partly on the understanding that the church would be left alone. But gradually Hitler interfered more and more in the life of the church. Eventually **Pope Pius XI** protested in an encyclical in 1937. In 1941 **Cardinal Galen** attacked the Nazi government for its abuse of human rights.

What of the Nazis themselves? Hitler disliked many of the ideas of Christianity and had no intention of giving the churches permanent protection. When the churches began to criticize him he became more extreme. The Nazis had always had a liking for **pagan festivals** (see Source E). Hitler gave permission for a pagan anti-Christian organization to be set up. This was called the **Faith Movement** and produced a journal called *Sigrune*. By 1941 most Nazi leaders were speaking in terms of destroying Christianity altogether.

SOURCE A

'Christianity is the unshakeable foundation of the moral and ethical life of our people.'

Hitler speaking to the Reichstag, 1933.

SOURCE B

'The Catholic people welcome the National Revolution, because the National Movement wants an end to unemployment, wants the economic recovery of the Fatherland and, above all, it wants the spiritual revival of the nation.'

A Catholic bishop welcomes Nazi rule, 1933.

SOURCE C

Nazi banners in a Protestant church, 193

SOURCE D

'From this community of German Christians there shall grow a German Christian National Church embracing the entire people in a National Socialist state of Adolf Hitler. One Nation! One God! One Reich! One Church!

The purpose of the German Christian Movement, December 1933.

SOURCE E

A pagan harvest festival, 1933.

SOURCE F

'We declare that the constitution of the German Evangelical Church has been destroyed. Its legally constituted organs no longer exist. The men who have seized the church leadership have divorced themselves from the Christian church.'

Some of the Protestant churches reject the German Christian Movement.

SOURCE G

'The concepts of National Socialism and Christianity are irreconcilable.'

Martin Bormann, Hitler's deputy, 1941.

2.12 SUPPORT AND OPPOSITION

EMPATHY

Support for Hitler and the Nazis

After 1933, support for Hitler and the Nazis grew. There were plenty of reasons for this. Hitler could be seen as the saviour of the German nation. He had brought unemployment down, ended the Depression and given Germany back its pride. Between 1936 and 1939 he also expanded Germany's frontiers and achieved a number of brilliant successes in his foreign policy. Propaganda showed Hitler as powerful and masterful and yet as good and kind to children. Most Germans would not have recognized the monster we now know him to have been.

Some may have had their doubts, though. They may have wondered whether it was right to destroy the opposition parties, to pack the Reichstag with Nazis, to end the free trade unions and to persecute the Jews. In addition, was it really necessary to rearm so quickly and to run so many risks in 1938 and 1939 of starting a war? Remember, however, that these doubts could not easily be expressed. Anyone speaking his or her mind might well end up in the hands of the Gestapo. This could mean prolonged questioning, torture and imprisonment in a concentration camp. How many people would be prepared to expose themselves or their families to this?

Opposition to Hitler and the Nazis

Once the war started those people who *were* courageous enough to oppose the regime faced a real problem. Although they hated the Nazis and everything they stood for, to go against the leaders of the nation was an act of treason. The German resistance was not the same as the French resistance which developed after 1940. The latter were patriots, while the former were seen as traitors and were detested even by moderate Germans.

Some Germans opposed Hitler from the very beginning. They were mainly Socialists and Communists, who tried to organize the workers in the factories. Others were originally prepared to co-operate with Hitler but then changed their minds. The author of Source A, **Ulrich von Hassell**, was the German ambassador in Rome during the 1930s and therefore a supporter of Hitler's policies. By the end of 1939, however, he had come to the conclusion that Nazi rule had damaged Germany in many ways. Later, in 1944, von Hassell took part in a plot to kill Hitler and end the Second World War. This failed, and Hassell, along with other conspirators, was sentenced to death and hanged. Although the church had made an agreement with the Nazis in 1933 (see pages 42–3), it eventually began to speak out against the way they abused human rights (Source B).

We now know that the worst atrocities were committed in the **concentration camps**. The SS tried to keep the extermination programme secret, probably because Himmler feared that the German public would be revolted by it. When British and United States troops entered these camps in 1945 they made local people bury the dead so that they could see exactly what had been done by the Nazi regime (Source D).

SOURCE **A**

'Among well-informed people in Berlin I noticed a good deal of despair. The principal sentiments are: the conviction that the war cannot be won by military means; a realization of the highly dangerous economic situation; the feeling of being led by criminal adventurers; and the disgrace that has sullied the German name through the conduct of the war in Poland, namely the brutal use of airpower and the shocking bestialities of the SS, especially towards the Jews.'

Ulrich von Hassell describes the feelings of some people in Berlin, October 1939.

SOURCE **B**

These numerous unexplained deaths of mental patients do not occur of themselves but are deliberately induced, and . . . in this matter the doctrine is being followed which maintains that one may destroy so-called 'lives which are not worth living' – a shocking doctrine which sets out to justify the murder of innocent people.'

Cardinal Galen objects to the Nazi programme of euthanasia, 1941.

SOURCE **C**

'We have to put a stop to the idea that it is a part of everybody's civil rights to say whatever he pleases.'

Hitler, in conversation on 22 February 1942.

SOURCE D

US troops make German civilians bury Jewish remains in Landsberg concentration camp, 1945.

SOURCE E

'In the autumn of 1936 I was expecting my second child. Hitler had been in power for three and a half long years, and, although we were becoming accustomed to some aspects of his regime, we were also beginning to realise we were living with a dubious dilemma. There was nothing to prevent us showing our disapproval by a lack of co-operation in as many small ways as we considered possible without risking our necks, and we had learned to watch out for the signs, the subtle signs from others who were doing the same. We could talk, therefore, with like-minded friends, and with them register amazement and also disgust. We knew no Nazis at all intimately, since to have done so would not only have been distasteful but also risky. Hitler had not long been in power when a very unpleasant phenomenon appeared on the scene: the informer who was not always a member of the Party, but who was none the less eager to show loyalty by reporting everything he saw or heard.'

Christabel Bielenberg, 'The Past is Myself', 1968.

EXERCISE

1 How do you think the Nazi leaders would have felt if they knew that people like the Bielenbergs were afraid to speak their mind? Explain your answer.

2 Christabel Bielenberg went on to describe her gardener, Herr Neisse, as 'friendly, gentle, even a little diffident'. How do you think he would have felt about the Nazi State?

3 What feelings about Nazi Germany do you think the Germans in Source D would have had? Give reasons for your answer.

2.13 OTHER NAZI LEADERS

The Third Reich was the creation of Adolf Hitler. It was, however, operated by a number of unscrupulous men who contributed in various ways to upholding the Nazi regime.

Hermann Goering

An impressive and popular figure, **Goering** was for a while the most influential man in Germany after Hitler. He was also the most versatile and had a hand in almost everything.

The first part of his career – up to 1941 – was remarkably successful. He had an aristocratic connection and achieved fame as an air fighter ace in the First World War. He brought some respectability to the early Nazi movement, becoming in 1932 Speaker and then President of the Reichstag. In 1933 he was one of the three Nazis in Hitler's first government and played an important part in setting up the Nazi police state. He secured from President Hindenburg the emergency decrees which damaged the other parties during the 1933 election campaign and gave special instructions to the police to deal severely with Communists. He also set up the Gestapo in Prussia and the first concentration camps, including Dachau in Bavaria. Meanwhile, as Air Minister, Goering founded a new air force, the **Luftwaffe**, in 1933. He directed the Four-Year Plan (1936–40) which was intended to prepare Germany for war. In recognition for his many achievements, Hitler gave Goering the title of **Reichsmarshal** in 1940.

Then gradually, Goering lost his influence. He was hated and envied by the other Nazi leaders and also did himself great harm through his addiction to drugs. Above all, Hitler blamed him for the failure to defeat Britain and the Soviet Union and also for the Allied bombing of Germany. His influence had almost disappeared by 1945. He was eventually captured by the Allies, tried at Nuremberg for war crimes and sentenced to death in 1946. Goering avoided the hangman by taking poison on the night before his execution.

Joseph Goebbels

More than anyone else, **Goebbels** was responsible for organizing **propaganda** in the Third Reich. He was a brilliant speaker, probably the equal of Hitler, and knew how to make the most of the medium of the radio to reach every German home.

Goebbels joined the Nazi Party in 1922 and was made head of propaganda in 1929. In 1930 he was elected to the Reichstag, and between 1933 and 1945 he was Hitler's Minister of Enlightenment and Propaganda. He was violently anti-Semitic and organized the destruction of Jewish property in the Kristallnacht of 1938 (see page 35).

During the Second World War, Goebbels constantly urged the German people to greater effort. He was made Chief Commissioner for Total Mobilization in 1944. But he was unable to prevent Germany's defeat and in April 1945 committed suicide, one day after Hitler.

SOURCE **A**

Herman Goering.

SOURCE **B**

Joseph Goebbels.

Reynhard Heydrich.

Reynard Heydrich

Heydrich was Himmler's subordinate. He was far more striking in appearance and was the only Nazi leader who actually resembled the 'ideal' German type – with blond hair, a narrow face and blue eyes. He too was utterly ruthless, but, unlike Himmler, was not squeamish.

In 1936 Heydrich was made head of the **Gestapo**, under Himmler's overall authority. In 1941 he became responsible for the details of the extermination of the Jews and organized their deportation from all over Europe to the death camps. In the same year he became governor of Bohemia, a territory taken by Germany in 1939. He might have emerged as Hitler's successor. In 1942, however, he was assassinated in Prague by Czech freedom fighters.

Heinrich Himmler

Himmler was one of the most contradictory of the Nazi leaders. On the one hand, he was insignificant and characterless; he was also squeamish about seeing people shot and was completely opposed to the hunting of animals. On the other hand, he became utterly ruthless and after 1934 he was one of the most powerful men in Germany. He had absolutely no feelings of guilt and was directly responsible for the deaths of millions.

Himmler's first taste of power came in 1929, when he was put in command of the recently formed SS. In 1934 his move upwards was accelerated as he helped destroy Röhm and the leadership of the whole SS and Gestapo network. His rise continued even while other Nazis, like Goering, were experiencing disgrace.

Himmler used his power in a way which will never be forgotten. He set up the **death camps** and supervised the means by which over 6 million people were exterminated. He decided, however, that the details of this should be kept secret, and they did not emerge until the **Nuremberg trials**. By this time Himmler was dead. In 1945 he deserted Hitler and tried to do a deal with the Allies. He was captured by the Americans in April and committed suicide by biting a poison capsule.

Heinrich Himmler.

Rudolf Hess.

Rudolf Hess

Hess was Hitler's earliest and most loyal supporter. He first became a follower as a student and was willing to suppress his own opinions and judgement, believing fervently in all Hitler's ideas. Imprisoned with Hitler in Landsberg Castle for his part in the Munich *Putsch*, he wrote down the first part of *Mein Kampf* from Hitler's dictation. As a reward for his loyalty, Hitler made Hess deputy leader of the Nazi Party in 1933. He was shy and introverted, content to remain in Hitler's shadow. His main function was to announce Hitler at meetings and rallies. He was very different from other Nazi leaders, who were very ambitious and sought to build up their own position.

In 1941 Hess flew to Britain on a strange peace mission which he dreamed up without Hitler's knowledge. He was imprisoned for the rest of the war and eventually put on trial at Nuremberg in 1946. He was sentenced to life imprisonment in Spandau Prison, where he remained until he committed suicide in 1987.

3.1 GERMAN FOREIGN POLICY, 1933–8

Cautious beginnings, 1933–5

For the first three years in power, Hitler was very careful in his foreign policy. He wanted to be considered a peacemaker rather than a warmonger. He wanted to increase his power *within* Germany first, and take no chances while Germany was building up its military strength.

In 1933 Hitler made his first major move by withdrawing Germany from the **Disarmament Conference** and the **League of Nations**. This made it clear that Germany intended to rearm, but Hitler also wanted to prove that he was not contemplating war. In 1934, therefore, he signed a **non-aggression pact** with **Poland**, by which the two countries agreed not to attack each other. This seemed to demonstrate that Germany had no hostile intentions against its neighbours.

Even so, Germany still had problems at this stage. In 1934 the German air force, the **Luftwaffe**, was set up. This angered Britain, France and Italy, which joined together in the Stresa Front of 1935. Germany seemed to be alone and vulnerable.

Gathering pace, 1935–7

During this period Hitler decided to move more quickly. Because rearmament was well under way he was now prepared to take more chances.

In 1935 both France and Czechoslovakia made treaties with the Soviet Union. Hitler had two answers to this. First, he made a **naval agreement** with **Britain** which allowed Germany to start building warships but allowed Britain a huge superiority in naval power.

Second, he tore up the Treaty of Versailles by sending three battalions of German soldiers to reoccupy the **Rhineland** (Source B). This was a considerable risk. The German High Command advised against the measure, as they expected immediate French resistance. Hitler later admitted that, if this had taken place, the German troops would have been forced to pull back. But nothing happened. Neither Britain nor France wanted to take any action which might result in a war with Germany. As a result, Hitler achieved a spectacular success.

Hitler's policy proved generally popular with the German people. Source B shows German troops being welcomed by civilians in Cologne, while a referendum confirmed that 98.8 per cent of Germans approved.

The remilitarization of the Rhineland had important results. The French were now weaker militarily, while the Germans were able to start work on their own fortifications in the west, the **Siegfried Line**. The event showed, above all, that a bold policy could pay off.

In 1936 Hitler went further. He took Germany into an agreement with Italy, forming the **Rome–Berlin Axis**. This was the idea of the Italian dictator, **Mussolini**. Hitler also set up the **Anti-Comintern Pact** against the Soviet Union, which was joined in 1936 by Japan and in 1937 by Italy. Germany was no longer isolated, and Hitler could move on to the next stage.

Goebbels (centre right) with the Polish leader, Pilsudski (centre left), at the time of the Nazi-Polish pact, 1934.

German troops in the Rhineland city of Cologne in 1936.

Union with Austria, 1938

Hitler had always intended to unite **Austria** with Germany. Two things stood in his way: Italy and the Treaty of Versailles, which forbade any union (known as *Anschluss* in German). The first problem was solved because Mussolini was involved in wars in Abyssinia and Spain and therefore lost interest in Austria. As for the second problem, Hitler again decided to defy the Treaty of Versailles at the earliest opportunity.

Throughout the 1930s the Austrian Nazis had been stirring up trouble for the Austrian government. In 1934 they assassinated the Austrian Chancellor, Dollfuss. In 1938 his successor, Schuschnigg, tried to persuade Hitler to guarantee that Austria would remain independent. Hitler's reply was to force Schuschnigg to appoint a Nazi, Seyss Inquart, to the important post of Minister of the Interior. Schuschnigg feared that Austria would soon be swallowed up by Germany. He therefore announced a referendum to give Austrian voters the chance to confirm that they wanted Austria to continue as a separate state. This was cancelled on Hitler's orders. Schuschnigg resigned, and Seyss Inquart became Chancellor in his place. The first thing he did was invite Hitler to send German troops to take over Austria.

The Anschluss proved extremely popular in both Germany and Austria. To Austrians it gave the chance of belonging to a major power once again. However, Austria suffered badly from its union with Germany. It was forced to give up its gold reserves and to allow its economy to be geared to the German war machine. It was purged by the SS and Gestapo, and Austrian Jews were persecuted from the start of German rule.

Again, Hitler's calculation that the Allies would do nothing was correct. France was going through a crisis of leadership and Britain again felt that Hitler's demands were not entirely unreasonable. For the second time in two years it was being argued that the Treaty of Versailles might perhaps have been too harsh. How much longer could this continue to happen?

Europe between 1933 and 1938. ▶

3.2 TOWARDS WAR, 1938–9

CHANGE

If you look carefully at diagrams **a** and **b** you will see some similarities and some differences between them. The differences are especially important. There was a major change in the relations beween the powers, which contributed to the outbreak of war in 1939.

1938 and appeasement

At first there were close links with previous policies, and *continuity* seems more obvious than *change*. In 1938 Britain and France were following a policy of **appeasement** towards Hitler. This meant that they let him have whatever they considered necessary for the preservation of peace in Europe. They felt that Hitler had certain definite aims and that once he had achieved these he would be satisfied.

We saw on pages 48–9 that Britain and France did nothing to prevent Hitler from remilitarizing the Rhineland in 1936 and annexing Austria. In 1938 another crisis arose. This occurred over the **Sudetenland**, a border area of **Czechoslovakia** which contained 3.5 million Germans. Hitler insisted that the Sudetenland should be given to Germany and threatened to go to war over it if necessary. President Beneš of Czechoslovakia asked France and the Soviet Union for help. The USSR would do nothing without France, and the British Prime Minister, Chamberlain, persuaded the French to keep out of trouble. He feared that, if any country assisted Czechoslovakia, Europe would be plunged into war.

Chamberlain took on the role of peacemaker, visiting Hitler three times. Eventually, in September 1938, Chamberlain, Hitler, Mussolini and the French Prime Minister, Daladier, signed the **Munich Agreement**. This gave Hitler the Sudetenland. In return, Hitler gave Chamberlain a written promise, or guarantee, that there would be no war. Chamberlain was now certain that there would be no more demands.

1939 and war

Within less than a year, two major changes had taken place. First, Britain and France abandoned appeasement and decided to stand up to Hitler. Lord Halifax explained the reason for this (Source A). Hitler, it now appeared, had gone beyond his original aim of absorbing only Germans into the Reich. In March 1939, for example, he had invaded and taken over the rest of **Bohemia**. This was certainly not intended in the Munich Agreement, and for the first time Hitler was now taking over *non-*Germans. When he started to demand land from **Poland** (Danzig and a Polish 'corridor'), Britain and France promised Poland support (see diagram **b**).

Hitler did not believe that Britain and France were serious, and he now intended to go ahead with an invasion of Poland (Source B). He did, however, take a precaution; this was the second great change of 1939. In August the German Foreign Minister, von Ribbentrop, signed a **non-aggression pact** with the Soviet Union (Source C), by which Germany and the USSR agreed not to go to war with each other.

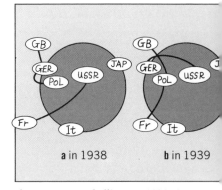

Agreements and alliances, 1938–9.

SOURCE A

'In his actions until after Munich a case could be made that Herr Hitler had been true to his own principle, the union of Germans in, and the exclusion of non-Germans from, the Reich. Those principles he has now overthrown, and in including eight million Czechs under German rule he has surely been untrue to his own philosophy. Are we to believe that German policy has thus entered upon a new phase? Is German policy now to be directed towards domination over non-German peoples?'

Lord Halifax in the House of Lords, 20 March 1939.

SOURCE B

'The objective is the elimination and destruction of military forces in Poland, even if war breaks out in the west. The quicker we achieve victory in the east the more chance there will be of limiting the conflict.'

From a report on Hitler's speech to his commanders-in-chief, 22 August 1939.

CHANGE

SOURCE C

'Both parties obligate themselves to desist from any act of violence, any aggressive action, and any attack on each other, either individually or jointly with other Powers.'

Article 1 of the Nazi–Soviet Non-Aggression Pact, 23 August 1939.

They also secretly agreed to divide Poland between them. The pact showed that **Stalin** had also changed his mind. Before 1939 he had hoped that Britain and France would stand firm in resisting Hitler. Now he too believed that they would do nothing; therefore he made his own arrangements with Germany. The pact came as a terrible blow to Britain and France.

Hitler now considered it safe to invade Poland, and German troops crossed the border on 1 September 1939. Much to the Führer's surprise, Britain and France declared war on Germany on 2 and 3 September. On 4 September, Chamberlain tried to explain to the German people why he had changed his mind so dramatically since 1938 (see Source D).

SOURCE D

'He (Hitler) gave his word that he would respect the Locarno Treaty; he broke it. He gave his word that he neither wished nor intended to annex Austria; he broke it. He declared that he would not incorporate the Czechs into the Reich; he did so. He gave his word after Munich that he had no further territorial demands in Europe; he broke it. He gave his word that he wanted no Polish provinces; he broke it. He has sworn to you for years that he was the mortal enemy of Bolshevism (the Soviet Union); now he is its ally.'

Prime Minister Chamberlain explains in a radio broadcast to the German people why he has declared war, 4 September 1939.

EXERCISE

1 Using the material on pages 48–51, construct a timeline from 1933 to 1939 which shows the major events in German foreign policy.

2 Chamberlain claimed to be working for peace. Was it a change in British policy when he did not welcome the Nazi–Soviet Non-Aggression Pact which aimed to preserve peace beween these two countries? Give reasons for your answer.

3 Are there any important differences between the Munich Agreement and the pact quoted in Source C?

4 Had British foreign policy changed between Halifax's speech (Source A) and Chamberlain's broadcast (Source D)? Give reasons for your answer.

5 Does Hitler's foreign policy between 1938–9 show change or continuity?

SOURCE E

'We were so engrossed in our plans during that summer of 1938, and we had become so accustomed to the explosive headlines, that we failed to grasp the full significance of the horror stories as they progressed from some humble position on the back page of the newspaper to blazing two-inch headlines on the front. "Pregnant Sudeten German mother pushed off bicycle by Czech sub-human in Ostravia!" "How long must our patient German brethren submit to such humiliating atrocities?" "The German people, united as one behind their Leader, can wait no longer." We'd had it all before, *ad nauseam* . . .

'When we arrived in Berlin in February 1939 the rumour was Hitler was preparing for war in the autumn. Poland would follow, it would not be long before we would be reading of Polish atrocities, Polish sub-humans.'

Christabel Bielenberg, a Briton married to a German, writing in her autobiography.

3.3 WAS WAR INEVITABLE?

EVIDENCE

In this unit we consider whether the outbreak of the Second World War was or was not inevitable. We start with a brief survey of Hitler's own attitude to expansion and war.

Hitler's statements

Hitler's views can be seen in four of the sources. The main one is *Mein Kampf* (Source A), written in 1925. Hitler wrote his *Second Book* in 1928 (Source B), although this was never published in his lifetime. In 1937 he held a secret meeting of his army commanders and revealed his intentions to them. One of the Nazi officers, Colonel Hossbach, took notes on the meeting; these came to be known as the **Hossbach Memorandum** (Source C). By 1945 Hitler had produced his last **Testament** (Source D).

Hitler's intentions

Two very different assessments have been made of what Hitler's true intentions were.

Many people believe that the Second World War was the logical and only possible result of Hitler's policies and that he fully intended it. Source E, for example, is part of the verdict at the Nuremberg Trials held in 1946 to deal with Nazi war criminals. Some historians agree with this assessment (Source F). After writing down his aims in the 1920s, according to this view, Hitler started to carry them out deliberately in the 1930s. War was therefore inevitable. Nazi plans for conquest and expansion could not have resulted in anything else.

An alternative argument is that Nazi Germany did not want a major conflict and that the outbreak of the Second World War was largely accidental. Some historians suggest that Hitler's ideas about conquest and expansion should not be taken too seriously (Source G). Also, Hitler did not move step by step towards a fixed target. Instead, he experimented and took risks. At first he was very successful but he was caught out in 1939 by a change in British policy (see pages 50–1).

Finally, some have argued that Chamberlain was partly responsible for the outbreak of the Second World War. He let Germany pursue its policies in 1938, believing that this was the best way to keep the peace (Source H). Then, in 1939, he suddenly changed his mind. Hitler did not believe him and went ahead with his invasion of Poland.

SOURCE

'We National Socialists must hold unflinchingly to our aims in foreign policy, namely to secure for the German people the land and soil to which they are entitled on this earth . . . If we speak of soil in Europe today, we can primarily have in mind only Russia and her border states.'

From 'Mein Kampf', 1925.

SOURCE

'Germany tries anew to champion her interests through the formation of a decisive power on land. This aim presupposes great military power but does not necessarily bring Germany into conflict with all European great powers.'

From Hitler's 'Second Book'.

EXERCISE

1 Is Source E a primary or a secondary source?

2 Do you think historians working on the causes of the Second World War will find Source E a useful source?

3 Does Source A provide reliable evidence to support the argument of either Source F or Source G? Explain your answer.

4 Compare Sources A, B and D. Do they suggest that historians will have to be suspicious of the reliability of all Hitler's writings?

5 Are the sources here sufficient to allow you to decide whether the argument in Source F or Source G is more likely to be correct? Give reasons for your answer.

EVIDENCE

SOURCE C

'Our relative strength would decrease in relation to the rearmament which would be carried out by the rest of the world . . . the world was expecting our attack and was increasing its counter-measures from year to year. It was while the rest of the world was still repairing its defences that we were obliged to take the offensive.'

From the Hossbach Memorandum, 1937.

SOURCE D

'It is untrue that I or anyone else in Germany wanted war in 1939.'

From Hitler's Political Testament, 1945.

SOURCE E

'The Tribunal is fully satisfied by the evidence that the war started by Germany against Poland on 1 September 1939 was most plainly an aggressive war.'

The Nuremberg Judgement, 1946.

SOURCE F

'But the fact is that those plans are unmistakably stated in *Mein Kampf* and that all the evidence of the 1930s showed that Hitler still intended to carry them out.'

Historian Hugh Trevor Roper, writing in 1961.

SOURCE G

'Hitler's exposition (explanation of his policies) was in large part day-dreaming, unrelated to what followed in real life. There is only one safe conclusion to be drawn. Hitler was gambling on some twist of fortune which would present him with success in foreign affairs, just as a miracle had made him Chancellor in 1933. There was here no concrete plan, no directive for German policy in 1937 or 1938. Or if there was a directive, it was to wait upon events.'

Historian A. J. P. Taylor, writing in 1963.

SOURCE H

Chamberlain promises peace after Munich, 1938. He is waving Hitler's 'guarantee'.

3.4 GERMANY'S CONQUESTS, 1939–41

Between 1939 and 1941 German armies conquered much of Europe. The main method was the **blitzkrieg** or 'lightning war'. The intention was to defeat the enemy as swiftly as possible. This could be done by surprise attacks. Bombers would be sent out to 'soften up' the main targets, followed by German **panzer divisions** – that is, tanks. Altogether, the Nazis launched five separate invasion attacks in Europe (see diagram).

Poland, September 1939

The first victim was **Poland**, invaded on 1 September 1939. Hitler sent in Stukas (dive-bombers) to attack Polish cities and destroy the Polish air force on the ground. You can see an example of a Stuka in Source A. Once control over the air had been established, the panzer divisions followed (Source B).

The Poles fought bravely but they had to rely on completely outdated methods. Their main forces were cavalry (Source C), which of course stood no chance against German tanks and aircraft. The conquest of Poland was completed within weeks. This was made even easier for Germany because the Soviet Union invaded Poland from the east. Neither Britain nor France was in any position to send help to the Poles.

Denmark and Norway, April 1940

Hitler then turned on **Denmark and Norway**. He intended to give Germany control over the long coastlines of the North Sea and North Atlantic. This was so that German U-boats, or submarines, could operate in the whole Atlantic area. In April 1940, using combined land, air and sea operations, the Germans conquered both countries.

The Low Countries and France, May and June 1940

Between September 1939 and May 1940 there had been very little fighting in the west; this period is known as the **'phoney war'**. In May 1940, however, Germany launched a devastating attack which brought **Holland**, **Belgium** and **Luxembourg** to their knees.

The main objective was **France**. The French thought that they were safe behind the fortifications called the **Maginot Line**. But the Germans bypassed the line and invaded through the Ardennes, a hilly and forested area which was supposed to be impassable to tanks. Paris fell within weeks. Hitler placed Northern France under direct German occupation but allowed Southern France to remain independent as an ally; this is usually called **Vichy France** (see map).

Attempts to conquer Britain, 1940–1

Germany then launched **Operation Sea Lion** in an attempt to conquer **Britain**. Acting on Goering's orders, the Luftwaffe bombed British cities, and plans were made for a full-scale invasion. But by 1941 Hitler had met his first major set-back. The RAF won the **Battle of Britain** against the Luftwaffe, and Germany had to postpone its invasion plan. For the time being, Hitler turned his attention elsewhere.

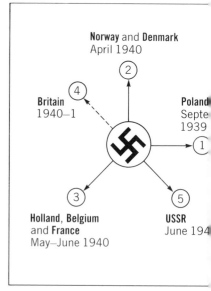

The main German invasions, 1939–41.

SOURCE **A**

Weapons of blitzkrieg: a Stuka over France, 1940.

SOURCE **B**

SOURCE **C**

The Polish response: cavalry in 1939.

Weapons of blitzkrieg: German tanks in Poland, 1939.

The invasion of Russia, 1941

In June 1941 Germany launched the largest invasion yet – **Operation Barbarossa** against the **Soviet Union**. Hitler thus broke the pact he had made with Stalin in August 1939.

Why did he do this? Part of the reason was that he wanted to deprive Britain of a possible ally. More important, he had never seen the Soviet Union as a permanent friend and intended, sooner or later, to destroy it. In this way he believed he would uproot communism and open up a huge area for Germans to occupy as **Lebensraum**. The Germans were extremely successful at first. By the end of 1941 they had conquered a huge area and captured or killed 3 million Soviet troops.

Europe by the end of 1941

The map shows the extent of Nazi Germany's victories by late 1941. Germany was now greatly enlarged and occupied countries to the east and west. Hitler had also taken **Greece** and **Yugoslavia** to the south and had the support of **Italy** and a number of other states. You can see how the Germans treated the conquered people of Europe on pages 58–9.

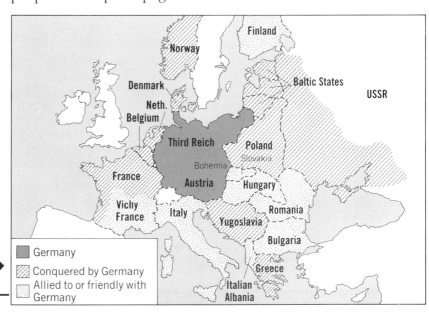

Europe under the Nazis. ▶

3.5 THE DEFEAT OF HITLER, 1942–5

CAUSATION

Nazi Germany reached the peak of its success at the end of 1941. In 1942, however, the tide began to turn. Between 1943 and 1945 the German armies were in retreat on three main fronts: the south, the east and the west. They were gradually driven back by the three Allies. One was **Britain**, which had been at war with Germany since 1939. Another was the **Soviet Union**, invaded by Germany in 1941. The third was the **United States**, which entered the war in 1941 – at first against Japan, and then against Germany.

The southern front

Hitler's ally, Mussolini, brought **Italy** into the war in 1940. Italian troops in **North Africa** were quickly defeated by the British, and Hitler had to send a German army under **Rommel** in February 1941. At first Rommel won a number of important victories. But in October 1942 he was defeated by the British at the **Battle of El Alamein**. Meanwhile, the Americans were also moving across to North Africa, and in 1943 the Allies were ready to move on to their next target: **Sicily**.

Churchill, now British Prime Minister, described Italy as the 'soft underbelly' of the Axis. British and US troops advanced rapidly from Sicily to the mainland, and in September 1943 the Italian government surrendered. Mussolini fled to the north, where he set up a small puppet state under German protection. He was captured and shot by Italian partisans in 1945.

The eastern front

The bitterest fighting and heaviest losses of the war occurred in the east. The Germans had cut through the Russian defences in 1941 but were eventually held at **Stalingrad**. Soviet and German troops fought for over a year in the rubble of the city, until in February 1943 the German commander, von Paulus, surrendered. Stalingrad was one of the most important battles of the Second World War and was followed by another Soviet victory in the tank battle at Kursk in July 1943.

From late 1943 onwards the Germans were driven steadily out of the Soviet Union. In 1944 Soviet troops liberated south-eastern Europe, and then Poland and Hungary. In spring 1945 Marshal Zhukov captured Berlin. Hitler committed suicide in an underground bunker within earshot of the Russian guns.

The western front

When the United States entered the war, plans were drawn up to invade **France**. It took some time to put these into action, but in June 1944 **Operation Overlord** was eventually launched. British and US troops, under the leadership of General Eisenhower, landed in Normandy and, two months later, in southern France. They gradually pushed the German armies back across the Rhine and in 1945 penetrated the Third Reich from the west as the Soviet forces entered it from the east.

Throughout 1943 and 1944 the RAF and US air force pounded German cities in a programme of **'saturation bombing'**. By 1945 the Third Reich was literally in ruins.

SOURCE **A**

An American playing card showing Hitler humiliated by the Soviet giant.

SOURCE **B**

	Tanks	Aircraft
Germany	9,300	14,700
USSR	24,700	25,400

Tank and aircraft production, 1942.

SOURCE **C**

'The Americans can't build planes, only electric ice-boxes and razor blades.'

Goering's comments on the US economy before 1941.

CAUSATION

SOURCE D

Soviet troops in Berlin, May 1945.

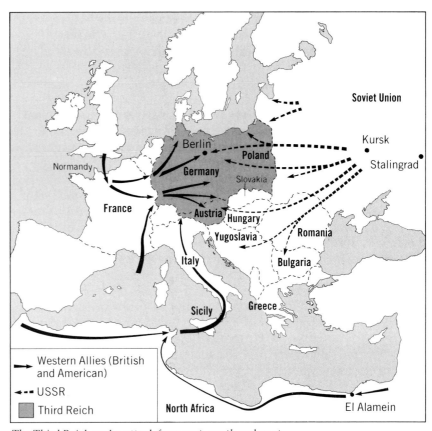

The Third Reich under attack from east, south and west.

EXERCISE

1 Does Source B give us a complete explanation of why the Soviet forces were eventually victorious on the eastern front? Explain your answer.

2 What was Britain's contribution to the defeat of Nazi Germany?

3 Is is true to say that the only important thing the United States contributed to the defeat of Hitler was to produce weapons and ammunition? Give reasons for your answer.

4 Which of the Allies do you think contributed most to the defeat of Germany: Britain, the Soviet Union or the United States?

5 Do you think Hitler may himself have been one of the causes of Germany's defeat? Explain your answer.

The strength of the Allies

Germany lost the war because it was overwhelmed by the greater strength of the three Allies. Britain, the smallest of the three, nevertheless controlled the seas and kept the war going during the difficult months of 1940–1.

The Soviet Union took the main brunt of the German attack and lost 25 million people. It did, however, have huge economic resources to fall back on and proved to be the giant shown in Source A. Source B compares Soviet and German armaments production in 1942.

The United States was completely underestimated by the Germans (Source C). In President Roosevelt's words, the USA became the 'arsenal of democracy' and produced a staggering amount of war material, including 300,000 aircraft and 86,000 tanks. Even with its allies (Italy and Japan), Germany could never hope to compete with this.

3.6 THE WAR CRIMES OF THE NAZIS

Throughout the Second World War the Nazis committed some of the worst atrocities ever known. The details of these did not become widely known until the trial of several Nazi leaders at **Nuremberg** in 1946.

Extermination of the Jews

In 1941 Hitler ordered Reynhard Heydrich to introduce the **'final solution'** to the 'Jewish problem'. The details were settled at a conference at Wannsee in 1942. A programme of mass slaughter was to be carried out at chosen centres.

Concentration camps had already been set up all over the Reich. Between 1941 and 1942 some of these were equipped with gas chambers and incinerators. These **extermination camps** were mainly in Poland and included **Auschwitz**, **Treblinka**, **Chelmno**, **Maidenek**, **Sobibor** and **Belzec**. To them were sent Jews and other people, including gypsies, from all over German-occupied Europe. Most of these victims died in the way described by the Auschwitz commandant, Hoess (Source A). Source B shows how the bodies were then disposed of, usually by other prisoners. It has been estimated that about 6 million Jews were killed during what is now known as the **Holocaust**. Medical experiments were also conducted, always without anaesthetic.

The people who committed these crimes, usually members of the SS, later said that they had been forced to obey orders (Source C). When not involved in their dreadful activities they appeared to live normal lives. Many of them had families and saw themselves as decent, law-abiding citizens. Most people today would find this double life very hard to understand.

SOURCE A

'I was ordered to establish extermination facilities at Auschwitz in June 1942. When I set up the extermination building at Auschwitz, I used Cyclon B, which was a crystallized prussic acid which we dropped into the death chamber from a small opening. It took from three to fifteen minutes to kill the people in the death chamber, depending on the climatic conditions. We knew when the people were dead because their screaming stopped. We usually waited about half an hour before we opened the doors and removed the bodies. After the bodies were removed our special squads took off the rings and extracted the gold from the teeth of the corpses.

'We received from time to time special prisoners from the local Gestapo office. The SS doctors killed such prisoners by injections of benzine.

'From time to time we conducted medical experiments on women inmates, including sterilization and experiments relating to cancer.'

Evidence of Rudolf Hoess to the Nuremberg Tribunal.

SOURCE B

The disposal of the victims of the gas chambers at Auschwitz.

'Unknowingly, I was a cog in the chain of the great extermination machine of the Third Reich.'

How Hoess later saw his role, from his autobiography 'Commandant at Auschwitz'.

'Upon my first visit I found these females suffering from open festering wounds and other diseases. They had no shoes and went about in their bare feet. The sole clothing of each consisted of a sack with holes for their arms and head. Their hair was shorn.'

The treatment of slave labour at the Krupp works: evidence given by Dr Jaeger at Nuremberg.

The main concentration camps.

The treatment of civilians

Eastern Europe was placed under the brutal rule of Hans Frank (the 'butcher of Poland') and Alfred Rosenburg. The Nazis considered the **Slavs** (Poles and Russians) to be an 'inferior race'; completely expendable, they could be worked to death. Slav workers transported to Germany lived in the worst possible conditions, as described in a doctor's report at Nuremberg.

The **SS** were directly responsible for killing millions of civilians in the occupied territories. Source E shows the hanging of five innocent Russians. There were also instances of mass shootings; in Kharkov in the USSR, the SS gathered together 100,000 civilians, ordered them to dig a trench and machine-gunned them into it.

SOURCE E

The execution of five Soviet citizens.

3.7 GERMAN CIVILIANS IN THE SECOND WORLD WAR

EMPATHY

You probably know people who experienced life as civilians in Britain during the Second World War. This unit tries to help you understand what it was like for the ordinary German.

Attitudes to the war

There was bound to be enthusiasm among German civilians during the first two years, as their armies won victory after victory. But from 1942 onwards the population began to experience greater hardship as the Allies fought back. The Propaganda Minister, **Goebbels**, called for a special effort and total loyalty (Source A). The tough talk and lack of easy promises are likely to have appealed to many German people.

Some, however, would have become more and more disillusioned, because **'total war'** meant a grim struggle for survival. Was this why Hitler had led Germany into war in 1939 (Source B)? A number of Germans regarded it as their patriotic duty to try to assassinate Hitler and end the suffering.

Rationing and shortage

While Germany was fighting the 'total war' referred to by Goebbels, the people faced increasing shortages, especially in food. As a result, **rationing** was introduced (Source C). To some this must have come as a shock, and there must inevitably have been complaints. Others, however, were probably willing to make sacrifices in the belief that they were helping conserve resources for troops at the front.

Source D gives evidence of black marketeering in Germany during the war. Again, attitudes must have varied. Some people became involved in the type of deals described, while others were outraged, regarding the black market as unpatriotic.

SOURCE C

A German civilian's daily ration of food: bread (12½ oz), jam (¼ oz), butter, fat, lard or bacon (1¼ oz), sugar (1¼ oz), meat (2½ oz if obtainable), coffee (¼ oz).

SOURCE A

'The British claim that the German nation has lost its faith in victory. I ask you: do you believe, with the Führer and with us, in the final, total victory of the German people? I ask you: Are you resolved to follow the Führer through thick and thin in the pursuit of victory, even if this should mean the heaviest of contributions on your part?'

Part of Goebbels' speech, 'Do you want total war?', 18 February 1943.

SOURCE B

'Everything is hollow, nothing but empty talk, theatrical gestures. The heroic battle of a nation for its ultimate possessions should look different. If the papers can write that this war is being fought for the sheer survival of German men and women, I must ask myself whether wars are fought for that. Surely sheer survival is no war aim.'

From a letter written by a German student to his father, 25 August 1944.

SOURCE D

'Farmers profiteeer, shopkeepers barter (butchers and drapers exchange meat and cloth), craftsmen carry out repairs where they are offered scarce goods . . . and officials dealing with the public receive gift parcels.'

Security report on black-market operations.

EMPATHY

SOURCE E

'Many German cities presented partial areas of vast devastation. Perhaps the outstanding example was Hamburg, where a series of attacks in July and August of 1943 destroyed 55 to 60 per cent of the city, did damage to an area of 30 square miles, completely burned out 12.5 square miles, wiped out 300,000 dwelling units and made 75,000 people homeless. German estimates range from 60,000 to 100,000 persons killed.'

Report from the United States Strategic bombing survey, 30 September 1945.

Bombing

The most terrible experience faced by most civilians was the destruction of their homes and cities from the air. In the first two years of the war the Germans were hardly affected. It was Poland, Holland and Britain which felt the main impact of bombing.

Between 1943 and 1945, however, most of Germany's cities were blasted by the RAF and the US air force. The destruction was massive, and hundreds of thousands of civilians were killed. This must have terrified many; yet, as in London during the Blitz, people learned to live with the destruction and tried to maintain their lives amid the chaos.

SOURCE F

Berlin after heavy bombing.

EXERCISE

1 Read Source A. How do you think Germans who heard Goebbels' speech reacted to it? Give reasons for your answer.

2 One of the aims of the German bombing campaign against Britain in 1940–1 had been to break the morale of the British. Do you think the use of bombing against German cities shows that the Allies thought this had worked? Give reasons for your answer.

3 How do you think people would have felt about the black market in Germany?

SOURCE G

Women civilians clearing rubble in Berlin. ▶

61

3.8 HITLER'S PLACE IN HISTORY

CAUSATION

The previous units on 'causation' looked at the cause and consequences of particular events. This time we reverse the process and consider the effect that Hitler had on events, both during his lifetime and after his death. We should also be able to see how important the individual can be in history.

Hitler's effect during his lifetime

Hitler had no effect on some of the events covered in this book. He did not, for example, have any influence on the defeat of Germany in the First World War, or on the Treaty of Versailles, or on the inflation of 1923, or on the depression after 1929. He used them, but he did not cause them.

On the other hand, Hitler can be held directly responsible for the changes described in pages 22–43. He created the SS, the Gestapo and the Nazi police state. His ideas were behind German rearmament, the tearing up of the Treaty of Versailles, the persecution of the Jews and the concentration camps.

There is a third way of looking at Hitler's influence. We can say that he played a crucial part in some events but that he was not *completely* responsible. One of the arguments on page 52, for example, is that he was not alone in bringing about the Second World War. As for his part in the war itself, he made some serious mistakes, mainly because he became overconfident (Source B). He insisted on planning the campaigns (Source A), often going against the advice of his generals. He therefore helped bring about the scene shown in Source D. Even so, a very important factor in Germany's defeat was the enormous strength of the Allies (see pages 56–7). Hitler could not have 'caused' this.

SOURCE B

'I do not doubt for a single second that we shall win in the end. Fate has not led me this far for nothing, from an unknown soldier to the Führer of the German nation, and Führer of the German army. She has not done this simply to mock me and to snatch away at the last moment what had to be gained after so bitter a struggle.'

Hitler expresses his belief in eventual victory, 1942.

SOURCE C

'Almost without transition, virtually from one moment to the next, Nazism vanished after the death of Hitler and the surrender.'

Historian J. Fest in his book 'Hitler', 1974.

SOURCE A

Hitler planning a military campaign.

CAUSATION

SOURCE **D**

Soviet soldiers place their country's flag on the Reichstag building in Berlin, 1945.

SOURCE **E**

A German civilian picking up a cigarette end, 1945.

Hitler's effect after his death

Great national and political leaders are remembered with love and respect. As for Hitler, most Germans seem only too anxious to block out his memory. Very few people are now influenced by Nazi ideas. By contrast, in the USSR Lenin continues to have a powerful impact more than half a century after his death.

Yet it could be said that Hitler's influence – unintended and indirect – *can* still be felt. As the main contributor to the building and then the destruction of the Third Reich, he made a great difference to the future of Germany and Europe. Germans suffered greatly after the war (Source E), and their country has ever since been divided between East and West. Also, in attacking the Soviet Union in 1941, Hitler helped unleash a devastating force which eventually placed most of Eastern Europe under Communist rule. Soviet victory in 1945 created a new superpower and set up the **Iron Curtain** in Europe.

Europe after 1945.

EXERCISE

1 List and explain four causes of why Hitler came to power.

2 How far was Hitler personally responsible for each of the four causes in your answer to question 1? Give reasons for your answer.

3 List and explain four important changes in Germany after 1933.

4 How far was Hitler personally responsible for each of the four changes in your answer to question 3? Give reasons for your answer.

5 a Do you think Hitler can be said to have been a cause of the scene in Source D? Explain your answer.

 b Do you think the scene in Source E might be said to be a consequence of Hitler's actions? Explain your answer.

6 Do you think the history of the twentieth century would have been different if Hitler had been killed during the First World War? Give reasons for your answer.

INDEX